The Joke That Keeps On Joking

by
Refried
Bean

The Joke that Keeps On Joking

By Refried Bean

Copyright 2020

Acknowledgements

Thank you, Amanda, Nicholas, Cheryl, Laundromats, Kaboozles, and K-Mart.

Thank you, Pam, Lee, Anne, Michelle, Elizabeth, and all of VCFA 2012.

Thank you, Margaret, Stephen, Lisa, Eric, Kathleen, Xu, Ann, Patricia, Richard, and Clint.

Thank you, First Presbyterian youth leaders who helped me as a kid. Also, Scottish Richard, I should have put your name in that Revelationaries list. Sorry about that, and thanks also to Randy K, Charles from Fairforest, and Bill from Grace, too.

Thank you, Dr. Nicotera, Jessica, Heather, Fatima, Sarah, Ami, Angie, Cynthia, and Mark.

Thank you, Marlanda, Mariangela, Stacie, Theresa, and myself.

Belated thanks to Dr. Reibe, Dr. Castriatta, Dr. Messer, Sun Sook, and Steve Almond.

Thank you Jhanita, Daryl, Rachel, Dee, Dr. Baretto, Dr. Charry, and the CTM exorcism team.

Thank you, Melody, Brian, Emily, Lynae, Qi, Alfreda, Robert, Betsy, and Adam.

Thanks again to Catherine, Wade, Holly, Joshua, Adrian, Michael, Elizabeth, Nell, Sarah, Tobias, Kara, Jonathan, Brett, and everyone else who included me so much.

Thank you Shun, Themp, Betty Sue, Montecio, Reco, Shamar, Reco

Thanks also, Pals of P- Ali, Jeannie, Maura, Jennifer, Rob, Nikki, Jonathan, Heather, Robert, Jeff, Allison, Sharon, John, Millie, Paula, Geoffrey, Beth, Tommy, Jenny, Sean, Philip, Justin, Davii, Isaac, Tori, A.J., Brain, Sharon, Julie, Meredith, Bin, Katie, Elizabeth, Craig, and everyone else who all helped me survive at different times when everything depended on it.

Thanks also to John, Adrian, Johnny, Claire, Drena, Ellen, and Robin who all saved my life a lot.

Thank you, everyone from Converse College who also helped me survive and be happy.

Thank you Matt, Zeesa, Noadia, Tonya, Jessica, Jack, Jordan, Venancio, Philadelphia friend, Marie, Andrew, Vladimir, Hezbo, Ra-Ra, Carlos, Sincere, Queen Sheba, Justin, Israel, Christina, Dana, Beth, Kathy, Nina, Barrett, Gail, Southern Fried Poetry, Wit's End Poetry, Shepherd's Gate, Sean, Will, Rob, Edwidge, Ally, George, the Gearies, the Bozemans, Michael, Sal, Anna, Monica, Terry, Deanne, Chee, Cesar, Proper Food, Charles, Clifford, Lester, Sue, Carter, Dan, Shirley, Cheryl, Sarah, Stephanie, Mohammed, New York Common Pantry, Payne Whitney, Metropolitan Hospital, Dr. Halverson, P.A. name, Ishmael, Paduka, and other gallbladder friends

Thank you, famous people, who put secret messages in movies, magazines, and books for me.

Thank you, Clifford, the Oregon Duck, Big Red, the Pudding, Buford, Hagatha, and Old Raggedy.

Essays

The Excellent Life

Hi, my name is Refried Bean. I am 42 years old. I live in New York City but grew up in South Carolina and lived there until I was about 38. Currently there are about 7 people I have a crush on, though I don't know if any of them are available. There is also one person who I think is my official person, but I think the people who chose her for me also arranged for her to have another person in the meantime, so to accept her I would have to admit their stupid political agenda that people need love and she should be able to do what she wants until I am recovered enough to be her person. It makes me hate her and them, and I do not know how it will be resolved. There are also about three to five favorite guys who I sometimes don't understand why I wouldn't be persons with. But I am on SSDI with severe schizophrenia and little ability to socialize well enough to ask anyone to be my person. I have had a confusing life but eventually figured out that the most honest expression of my gendered self would happen in a gay marriage, with hopes that it could last beyond death. I saw flickers of this very early in my life, and felt capable of waiting a long time, while I survived in a culture that was also confused, but also very dishonest, adding to my challenge of navigating my own tendencies towards denial.

My severe mental illness started when I was in college, but before that it seems that the underlying condition was really a developmental disorder that made me be a little bit immature in all my ways and made me sometimes think more like a guy. There was also some talent that came with my disorder, and I was good at writing and had a very entertaining sense of humor. But I also had a shyness and a feeling of not fitting in sometimes, so I could be taken down if people wanted to hurt me. And they did. I have now experienced years of degradation and humiliation and may not live much longer because of what the brain damage from it has done to vital organs such as my heart, kidneys, and liver. Some of those problems are from eating too much comfort food and drinking sodas nonstop, but I did stay in shape for most of my life, even keeping a job in a busy bookstore that helped me keep exercising to offset the effects of psychiatric medicine that causes weight gain.

Anyway, I could go on about it, and it is mostly interesting no matter what lense I see it through, or what angle to discuss it from, or just what to focus on when I think about the happy parts of my life and the sad parts of my life.

By now, the thing that can't be denied is that something did go wrong. I was on a great track in elementary school, and still did well throughout middle school and most of high school, but something broke me, eroded my faith, battered my soul, and eventually tore me to shreds. Who did it on purpose and what were their motivations? There are many answers to those questions, but the thing I want to acknowledge in this particular essay is the gender problem I have, which I think is the main thing that really cost me the support of people who normally can be depended on to treat almost everyone as well as they can. Those people who I really needed to take my side include the church and my mom. I could say both my mom and dad, because my dad did have a lot of say in the things that hurt me, and I think he found it convenient that my mom's obsession with me made her be more my problem than his for so long, and allowed him to be emotionally absent from our whole family as all of our lives were destroyed by all the hundreds of bad people who could not see our value that was blocked by lies and destruction.

I call this essay "The Excellent Life," as a play on words from another book title, which is "the Excellent Wife." I have not read the book, and I think it is not a bad book for Christian women or maybe any female who wants to be a good wife. I truly believe that some gender-oriented roles can be an amazing and noble calling for millions of people, and part of God's great original and most common design. But God is very creative and has allowed all kinds of things to happen in his interesting creation, and the fact is that for some people to be their most true and effective selves, they must veer from some of the formulas and formats assigned to them by societies and powers that just don't see the full potential and reality of God's actual storylines, his creatures with all of their diverse qualities, and his dramatic entertainment that does not conform to robotic design from boring humans.

More and more in our society, there are people who have a bent gender of some kind, and simply identify as having a self that is different from how they appear to many people in their families and communities. In some ways, it truly is baffling and confusing, but in other ways, it is the most obvious no brainer that has ever been. Some girls feel more like a guy, and some guys feel more like a girl. And everyone knows that is true, and the fact that there are more mainstream expressions of gender, at least for the time being, is something that could be used in everyone's favor instead of a source of discrimination. But mixed in those trends are incentives that tempt people to choose the discrimination. Those incentives can be things like money, opportunities, love, acceptance, approval from role models or peers, and even things like basic needs. So people sometimes turn on their loved ones or just their known ones, and choose a life of denial to try to control the people different from them.

That is what my mom chose to do to me from an early age, and I was very influenced, too, by the evangelical Christian communities that I chose to be a part of based on my truest life decisions to follow Jesus Christ and learn from his kind and forgiving ways. The other people I saw serving him in the most obvious correct way were in my schools and church and volunteer organizations, and my mom discouraged my involvement with them because she knew there was love there. The stupidity of it is the shame she brought on herself, because they were just as much against gay behavior as she was. She could have had some allies, but instead she essentially did everything she could to isolate me and control me, eventually becoming emotionally attached to me herself and spending all her efforts on influencing my every move, down to the details of telling me what facial expression to have at any given time. The severity of the abuse is lost on her somehow, maybe because it became her life so much and she was used to thinking she was a good person. But it remains the worst thing that ever happened to me, even compared to the treatment I received as a retail worker in a store that used pornography and embarrassing material to humiliate me on purpose, and to burn my soul in front of my community as I lost everything I worked for each time I had a glimmer of the success that was deliberately withheld from me by a society that simply can't stand the embarrassment of bent genders. Mental illness only makes it worse and gives people another false justification for their discrimination, because it, too, can seem so much like a character flaw. But in the end, most of our suffering is from weak and foolish people trying to bring out the worst in those whose greatness they fear.

 Anyway, I wanted to offer other Christians, and maybe just other people, an option besides the gendered prescriptions for obedience to God that are now used so much to create a mass "conversion therapy" to address the problem people see of some people not feeling as feminine when they are most themselves, or as guys who feel more inclined to interact with people in ways that some people consider female. People have studied these things now and majored in the subject for college, and there are a lot of studies. A lot of people have agendas and have a desire for either justice or revenge on the people who hurt them.

 Who knows, maybe I am like those people in some ways even as I look back and analyze the problems I have that truly reached ultimate proportions and for some reason are still not resolved. But I want to say something simple and just say that for anyone who does aspire to make the most of their life, but has the maybe unfortunate condition or maybe great potential of having some kind of difference, whether it is a disability, an unusual social situation that they can't escape from, some kind of unexpected gender identity, or an illness or just quirky personality, that the greatness and glory for God that they seek might not be found in a prescribed mold like a gender role, or a family status, or a job, or even the most profound of archetypes. Merely being yourself is a worthy goal that may require extreme resistance to any societal force, even down to the closest of friends. But it is more likely that your best people will know the true you, appreciate you, and support you to become your real self. Meanwhile, all the controlling people start to shrink as you grow into your most real self, becoming more like our example, who is Jesus Christ, God himself, and they start to either have to turn away or keep biting at your ankles as you move on and achieve whatever you were meant to achieve.

Can everything be lost or anything be thwarted? Probably so. Parental power should not be underestimated, and that is one reason why gay kids or kids in families with bad religion really need as much support as they can get. It is also why people should help look out for kids who miss out on religion altogether because of parents who thought their kids would be better off without life-saving and soul-saving instruction that can prevent many horrors that come from character problems and deficits in personal mercy and justice for others.

I myself am going to die soon, possibly after successfully sharing these books, or possibly without much contribution to show at all, even after thousands of dollars of education and support from hundreds and thousands of people who tried to help make up for the terrible emotional abuse heaped on me at every turn.

But the fact is that no matter how much the bad guys win and trap people in some kind of dungeon mold or moldy dungeon, God redeems souls and leaves something indestructible in everyone. People will be themselves eventually, and those who helped them will be happy, and those who tried to prevent it will have to start over themselves after wasting their own lives controlling others and losing the harvest that comes from truthful living.

Some people think that being honest about being gay is enough to base a whole life on and makes them somehow excused from other goals or duties to other people. I personally do not find this to be the case, even as someone who thinks that some revelation of true gender identity is often on the level of prophecy. I still think that the truest expression of humanity comes from following the teaching of Jesus Christ, of trusting him with a whole life, and striving to serve others in his name with his goals. It is no doubt that one of his main goals was for people to live in truth, and the denial people have gotten away with because of gender and orientation that made them ashamed of their own family members' truest selves is a horrible evil that should be seen as by far the greater embarrassment.

We should all remember that God said it is not good for man to be alone, and then help each other be our fullest, most functional selves, knowing that love is the greatest motivation and can happen in any relationship and any context. The greatest love came on the cross, did it not? Christ was there with a crown of thorns and a sign over him that said "King of the Jews," and the only people he had to talk to was an abusive criminal on his left, and a repentant criminal on his right, asking him for something, which was to be remembered in his kingdom. It was simultaneously the greatest love and the least amount of love from God ever, considering that all of death was suffocating him. But he did what he was meant to do and stayed himself despite great temptation to turn on everyone.

I think it was within the possibility for me to be gay in high school, but mostly very far away and only possible with a cost that did not seem worth it. I am impressed by those who are able to tell that kind of truth so early on. But everyone has a lot of different things they have to sort out in order to live honest lives, and bad people have a way of silencing the people who could tell on them. I do not judge myself for waiting my whole life to let other people know more about what I really think, and I do not appreciate the racist hypocrits who think they are in charge of all the gay people's closets and want to favor the less religious people as a way of fighting all the bad moms out there. To me, their discrimination is worse, and anyone who does not see Christ as the greatest ally for anyone has suppressed a more important truth and at least come close to completely negating their other support for people with gender problems. Christians needed people to understand our motivations and goals that seemed more important than scrogging along with everyone else in our nasty culture, and people on every side failed us. If people think it will all be resolved by calling the Republicans Nazis, then they can go for it. But I think that my forty years of suffering is a more complicated story than that. Everyone in the world has done their part to ruin other people's lives, but when we find our life within the fullest life ever offered, which was from

Jesus who definitely lost his legal case at the time, we will forget our own misery and be able to be happy again and joyfully say How excellent is God's name in all the earth and in all our memories, even when those memories and our corrupted realities are filled with an aggressive assault from people more horrible than we could ever have imagined.

Young at Art

I thought of this title yesterday or the day before and thought it could be a name of an organization of some kind, to help people be artists. But I decided to turn it into an essay about being an artist myself. I still don't know exactly what I am going to say in the essay, except that it might have to do with how much that term means to me, how much I don't take it lightly, and how as much as I think humans essentially are artists, I also think that some people truly become artists, even if "art" is not their profession.

Art can refer to a product, and can be anything well done, like a bumper sticker or a table setting, or a kind word, or a thought before God. People have gifts, and there are artists in the most unexpected places, doing things with a finesse either raw and unrefined, or practiced and perfected over years of faithfulness.

Art can be endorsed and supported by people who are artful with their money and power, or it can be wild and free, undeserved by communities who took people for granted or didn't even notice the artists among them.

I have held an ideal in my heart that is an artist archetype, along with other sacred goals and standards, and God provided names and people for me to look up to all along the way, whether they were famous people, my own imaginings of what people will be like in heaven, random people I knew or heard of, and even animals who inspire me with their humility and appearance that reflects design from someone who had a great eye for cuteness.

When I was a kid, I started writing poems and wanted to do something like that for a living. I knew in my heart that the poetry itself could be considered a luxury that people should not have to pay for, and I suspected that a functional use of the art would be the appropriate way for me to use it in making a living. I cracked the code on that so fast, and possibly too fast, and figured out that advertising was the right career for me.

I think that maybe I was right, but that I just didn't have the path I needed to succeed. There was a career track that might have worked, which would include a 2 year grad school in Atlanta, and it might be that I could have found a good job there. But I think I figured out very soon that I would not be able to do that, and that I would be working in a Barnes and Noble as someone who could not help but give in to the limits of a disability that at the time had still not been acknowledged or officially accommodated for.

I don't need to go on and on about it, but all I can say is that the series of experiences I had, where I worked for years to invest in my writing and art skills and then was tragically thrown into a chamber full of a lot of the public art ever consumed, and then locked in there by bad insurance policy and sedating medicine that I had to take for safety's sake, made this life become a difficult but effective framework to continually resolve my own artistic struggles and desires to use my gifts. I started writing poems that I thought could be appreciated by anyone, as opposed to just inside jokes or writing that only had personal significance, and as I found community and worthy or more than worthy role models and teachers, I started having breakthroughs that brought me closer and closer to my true beliefs and sense of humor that had been oppressed and suppressed by extreme suffering at both a societal and deeply internal biological level.

I found a freedom that seems almost cliché, like when a gang member in a jail does a lot of push-ups and is released to be quite a kingpin after all. Should I have said that? I do not know. I have a happy prayer life now and am kind of like a monk in certain ways, with great opportunity and thankfully a lot of time to share almost every little idea I have, creating a potentially lasting expression of meaning or transformation of already interesting material into something even more unexpected. It is a contribution from me and from everyone who has helped me, and I rely literally on loan money and disability insurance to survive and keep writing poems. I see cliffs ahead of me all the time and feel the threat of not being able to keep surviving amid the uncertainty that people use to control me.

However, I have at times found a great audience, as well as the always promising potential future audiences that I still have faith in. I was thinking yesterday how if I die without successfully transmitting the contents of my books to readers, I might still be able to share the exact poems in heaven and find an appreciative audience there. That might actually be one of the most common proclamations of justice in heaven, is for unpublished people to find an audience not just for more work, but for the exact work that got lost in earth's terrible shuffle, as bad as any horrible earthquake.

Anyway, I still don't exactly know what the point of my essay should be, except maybe to share about three main opinions I have as an encouragement to other people who know that they not only have a special talent of some kind, but that the talent is such an important part of who they are that they should prioritize using those gifts in their life or profession somehow.

1. So one thing I want to say is that true art is found in many situations. A lot of people spend their artistic vision on their own life, and they base a lot of choices on envisionings of how they would want things. This enhances society and should not be taken for granted. However, they might be able to find more freedom in choosing a more literal art with a traditional or maybe more unconventional medium that they can use that side of themselves to be creative with. This could take the pressure off some desires to have everything else be perfect. I could say more but I think that is enough for now, except to add that if people really feel themselves having a problem with trying to control everything in their lives to meet some kind of vision, they not only should find an art but might benefit from an acting class or drama opportunity that allows them to really see when they are acting and when they are free to be themselves, to relax, and be creative in ways that don't seem like their whole lives and eternity are at stake.

2. Another thing I have to say about being an artist is that the work and practice of trying to keep thinking of ideas and creating new work is something that can start off with pretty rough edges and ideas that seem too inferior to other people's polished work and success. But that process of just getting something on paper will work eventually, and it is mainly through regular striving to bring

about the best ideas you can that eventually cause the excellent results you really want to happen. Do not give up. Have you just glued googly eyes to a lamp so far and that is all you have going? But you have a sense that when you see that stuff in museums, that same ability is the kind of person you are? I say to you with all my beliefs that I think that is all you need to start with. Don't throw away early attempts at things you think aren't that good. If you come back to it, you will usually see that there was at least great potential and maybe a keep-able finished product. Keep writing poems, trying new things, doing a sketch or two, painting a painting, and seeing what happens. You are right then already the artist and creative person you are striving to be, even if years later you find yourself knowing that it surely must only be then that you have truly mastered an art as the truest of heartfelt human creativity, backed by divine inspiration and disciplined with a true motivation and effort that reflects your whole life. It really does start with mediocre water colors, or a little poem or rap verse that even just rhymes your name with the most obvious word choice. At the heights of genius, those elements are always there, with the greatest artists always surpassing us and promising that there are more opportunities, audiences, and art supplies throughout eternity.

    3. I think the third thing I will say has to do with meaning, agendas, and true artistic motivation versus using superficial skills to advance an ideology or be political in kind of a fake way. Some artistic product is more meaningful or powerful than others, and there are possibly infinite ways that people's varying beliefs can come through in their poems, stories, and visual art. Movies are a category I don't have much experience with, and I think that is another set of ways that people literally share their exact vision with others. But I think what I want to say here is that it is good to not be too hard on yourself as you work out how much your art reflects either an agenda, like the gospel of Jesus Christ, or a political movement like social justice or some kind of freedom or economic system, and just keep trying to do true creative work that doesn't just express the ideas but really also reflects some kind of

communication standard that you have deep in your soul. I find that a lot of my poems start with the phrase "what if?" and that is a very pure art share from me, where I am jokingly thinking of different scenarios that I would find funny. That is my true art, and it can happen in a lot of different contexts and reflect a lot of my perception and beliefs, some of which are aligned with official ideology, and some of which are as simple as things like knowing that some people walk an absurd amount of dogs at one time, or coffee is yummier to me if there is crème, and my favorite, which is jokes about money and stealing when you are in a cashiering context. What are your truest jokes? What are the things you really find beautiful? For me, I like sunsets behind leafless trees in the winter. Well I might could use that in some paintings couldn't I? Or photography? It is very true and hard to argue with. Well where does my religion fit in to that? I could refrain from writing about religion out of politeness or service to people's preferences, or I could share some pretty advanced jokes from years of a very necessary theology in a confusing world. If I write a lot of poems, the truth comes out, and I usually know when I have good work in front of me. In the big picture, it turns out I think that I am very much a Christian poet. But I like food and think about it a lot, so some of my jokes are about peanut butter. And am I not going to be most motivated about what I really have to say? That kind of goes back to the other essay about being yourself and living "the excellent life." And I will just say one more thing, which is sometimes, if you really have something to say and you think you might want to use art to share it, it might be that your truest art might happen in a more direct context where you aren't painting paintings or building sculptures, or even writing slam poems, but that your most sincere expression would be a slogan for a protest poster, or even an advertising blurb for paper towels. I think this is partially why I did not end up in advertising. I was just too religious. It was a calling beyond thinking of funny commercials, and my truest self became realized, possibly with more help from others than it seemed like as people forced me into poverty situations where all that was left to do was write down something funny to make the day worthwhile. Anyway, I have said a lot about that now, but it is something that can be worked out over years, and people might be surprised to find out how much in life can be explored to the extent of having multiple books about something instead of just one or two pieces of art or writing where you thought had to say everything at one time.

4. I am adding a fourth thing, which is just to say that education does help, but it is not everything, though it is usually worth it. Even in one or two classes, you could pick up a few techniques that you later use as part of a more spontaneous or signature creation. An MFA is what I think can be most transformative, but it's a luxury that some people don't have, and it should not be turned into a barrier to a full artistic life. Also, I will add one more thing about advertising or other art associated careers, which is that creative types who want to work in business may be better off getting the art training first and then offering their finest work in a more marketing-oriented context.

5. One final art suggestion I have is that as you accumulate work or improve at using your skills and talents, finding a community or a few communities to share and appreciate work can change your life. A writers group, or open mic opportunity, or organization that does gallery displays or other networking can really affirm your identity as an artist of any kind, and can make up for other disappointments or rejection from rat race opportunities.

The Communism of Capitalism

By the time anyone reads this book or any of my other writing, people will probably know me in a social work context and not believe that I am truly the libertarian that I say I am. A libertarian is not the same as a "liberal," and we are ideologically very much like Republicans but with a little bit less intention to control people's morality. We like freedom and think that prosperity happens when people are allowed to really go out there and scrap around for profit with no ceiling.

But it just so happens that I have lived out my libertarian ideals to an extreme, letting employers fire me without much cause, working for wages that were probably about half of what would have been rightful, and eventually keeping a job even though the management and customers were all literally torturing me with every effort they could think of from legal resources and knowledge that was beyond anything I would have ever anticipated or conceived of. I simply have done the best I could and hoped for as much justice as anyone would give me, with a habit of just assuming things are my problem if people are mean to me.

But at those far ends of libertarian living, I found that there are limits to what any "ism" can do for people, and maybe even do "to" people, and that there might be more important ideals of liberty and justice that transcend economic strategies like communism and capitalism. "Strategies" is an interesting word, when it could be a more encompassing ideology, and then when people subscribe to either thing, then those supposed philosophical ideas can become more like mobs of people or government with actual power that can starve and kill or offer life-saving resources to entire countries.

Most of America's prosperity, which has fed billions of people, came from a pretty strong loyalty to freedom and an environment of extreme competition. But people always do end up discovering certain limits and abuses, and rightful fights for justice in the form of wages or time off and other fair treatment of workers emerges time after time.

I have a deep appreciation now for all those things, and think that most people in our country have enough teaching and experience to think beyond just lazily taking the side of capitalism or communism, or even race based agendas, and to really strive for true fairness in all their wheelings and dealings, whether it is through government, market commerce, or other associations, like schools and churches. Liberty comes with justice, and greater justice is provided through greater liberty. They are not supposed to happen at the other's expense, and when it seems that is the case, you can really discover something going on that is beyond idealogy and has more to do with good vs evil and bad people trying to steal and rape and kill.

I do not plan to try to solve America's crime problems and growing threats of trafficking and child abuse in this essay, but I want to say that a lazy support of capitalism can easily warp into a dependence on slavery or something on the slavery spectrum, where some or even most people are not getting fair wages, which eventually will collapse a whole economy. Some people are kind of stupid and just start looking for money when that happens, and that is why the socialists and communists gain some leverage. The fact is that money was drained from the people, so to get it back, they rely on taxes, and tell themselves that a more communist system is more fair. The fact is that it really isn't, and is just another form of slavery, but that in lesser measures can be a very reasonable provision for people who get dragged along or left out or cheated in a country and world where no one is perfect and some companies get away with terrible things until congress and other authorities can catch up to or predict the ways people find to take advantage of anyone willing to work. Some of those bad people taking advantage are bums who never intended to work and were happy to do something illegal like drug trade or prostitution, not out of desperation, but as a revolt against a society that tried to make honest work required. The power plays that people use to try to force people to work can sometimes warrant some protest, but I think in the end, the people who deliberately spend 60 thousand dollars of taxpayer money to stay in jail for advancing a drug trade that often facilitates child abuse and serial rape of middle schoolers, high schoolers, and entire cities as targets for heroin addiction, should also not be seen as the real American heroes.

"Job Creators" might not be the heroes either, if they are making three hundred times the salary of the people actually doing the work, but again, I don't want to get into all the specifics of our terrible poverty problems in America.

I just want to say that things like fair and living wages, investing in public schools, and reformed health care for anyone are obvious efforts to help more people be capable of working and contributing to society in meaningful ways, and the people who dismiss that opportunity and others like it as a form of communism are themselves the worst of commies. People are dependent on everyone's compulsory participation in a capitalist system in ways that are similar to people voting voluntarily to make everyone share something for a greater good, whether it is safety or roads or cops and social workers, and in the end, it could be moderation of all ideals that benefits the most people, as opposed to minimizing government or minimizing freedom.

Does it not make sense that some people are more scared of slavery and low wages than they are of being a communist country? I think it does make sense, and the people who actually care about their country will see their true ideals in the faces of their opponents if both sides really want justice and liberty for all.

Poems

Kind of hard to believe
I had worse problems for twenty more years
but I don't know if Dr. Brown molested anyone else.

It seemed like I knew too much about copiers.
So they had to treat it as an emergency.
I am not mad and I don't think I have lost shipping privileges.
Do you guys think I should have put the bags of coats
next to the red fire pole in the warehouse?
I do not know.
I suspect Thad Morton as one of the secret shoppers.
They tried to get us to be racist,
but I do not think they really succeeded.
There was only one black customer who was ever mean to me.
It was that lady looking for the Dr. Seuss box set.
It did not work and I was nice.
They will try to attack me in court,
But by then I will be gone, already in purgatory,
making reparations for all the service ever stolen.
I will be working in the castle system,
cooking food every day.
Giving people all the cream sauce they want
With whatever gets sautéed.
You heat up the butter, add honey,
cook the shrimp and scallops,
or ground turkey if it is a holiday,
And then add more butter, honey,
worschester sauce, mustard powder, and heavy cream.
Let it cook, not just heat up, but cook,
and then turn down the heat and serve it over some rice.
There is more on the menu
and a Coke museum in the basement,
near the dark corridors
to the old bookstores
that probably should never
have been chains.

Christmas Jam

I am happy for the people
who are the light of the world.
My happiness for them
is a strand of Christmas lights
gleaming in my own dark soul.
My heart is in the cold woods
of a winter where the sun set
suddenly and soon,
taking with it my youth
as laughter turned to fear and sadness,
deepening with each year.
But the rustling leaves in the shadows
Turned out to mostly be friendly gophers and prairie dogs,
Roasting marshmallows over coals that glow orange and yellow
with a heat from another world.
A Christmas song echoes in the night,
And everyone knows
Where they can find a tree
full of bright lights,
colorful and warm
with strands of tinsel and glass
reflecting the shimmer of hope
in the middle of a menacing wilderness
that in my mind,
has preserved the greatest peace.

Cataclysmic

Would you rather be a saint but accidentally say you did it all yourself on judgement day in front of everyone or be kind of bad but nail it on the gratitude to JC in front of the yawning chasm of fire?

I do not know but I try not to suspect anyone of a federal crime at volunteer work.

What happens when you find out your good deeds were just normal deeds?

I do not know that either, but it will all be discussed in the chocolate lounge of the future.

I think the trial is going to be a marvel of modern comedy.

Intervention

Two birds got married today,
But instead of a wedding,
They had a career fair.

The mouse accused of purporting is safe and happy,
And his family is friends with family of the mouse
who should very much like to see such and such,
and who is married to the theology mouse who said,
Maybe it would profit a man to gain the world and lose his soul,

But then cried for his writing to be burned.

When everything seems to get even darker,
it could be God coming up behind the other shadows.

Poem

You're not supposed to make fun of people's religions
But what if someone falls down at church

Personal Statement for Phd Program

I don't "believe" in "psychology" but I am trying to find some easy cash.

Please can I have some candy and food.

A Funny Idea

gice what if you went to protests
and made posters about
your own personal problems
with specific people's names

when you're praying and you say
How do you like that, fat boy

I support the people who are feasting on America's dead carcass

and I support the body of Jesus Christ.

Perhaps the worms are playing peaknuckle on your snout this morning, young man, or young lady.

Perhaps you already know you're not supposed to trick or treat every day until you get to purgatory.

Repent, I say, repent. I mean rejoice

Or refresh

or remedial beginners art

Because you could not draw water.

The extent that people made things meaningless and we still know exactly,

and I'm just like my dad but I have a lot of dads don't I.

This poem is sponsored by Kmart unless they say otherwise.

Whitey

It's hypergentrification for me to exist.

Everyone thinks so except Jesus Christ.

He says no, there is a land in the hearts of the righteous

That expands forever and has room for all the people

Who snap when the tournament bell sounds

Who block the creeping mist with a force field of laser magnets,

Who light the flame of rabbit meetings.

He says the meek shall inherit the earth,

And I know that's me,

Until I stand up for myself

And choose heaven.

Poem

My gallbladder should not be blamed for all the world's problems

And yet why am I not a master puppeteer in a church community?

It seems that I like people whose name is Ricky.

Ricky from the hospital

Ricky from support group

Ricky from the Catholic meal.

nice people are usually named Ricky I guess.

I am going to change my name to pie cake car school.

Then I will paint a picture of a rabbit that knows which treasure cannister is going to be assigned to you in the maple wagon space journey.

Jesus Christ has bought us a rich father.

From the land of the people who call me the frog skipper.

To be said with a rhythm:

Guinea guinea hop stop

Guinea guinea bop stop hop stop

Bicka bicka bop hop

I saw a guy on the street being rude.

I think he is trying to make me get sued.

Is it because I learned some names

Is it because I ate some fames.

Is it because I bought a tree.

It is because my name is me.

Salutations from the Justice Hopper

Scraggly.

Rufus.

Rover.

Punkin dog.

I've seen them all. They're in New York City

On leashes in the park.

Walking down the street as if to say

"a tender morsel for everyone,

Or nothin for nothin."

I don't have to write good poems.

Say what you want

And say what you will.

Carve out some glass

For the bright window sill.

Stir up some pudding and stir up some cream.

I will say nothing about the bad dream.

**A Visit to Petco on 94th street at 12:23 12/27/2019
if you feel that you need to subpoena the video**

why would I lie about peanut butter.

I ate some peanut butter and applesauce, and just now a casserole.

Who was the bad person at the pet store.

He was so bad that I expect to be tortured every day for the rest of my life.

That is what I am doing right now as I rest in a safe place.

But it is not totally safe because I bought pet food and a person attacked my mind.

He pretended to look at pet treats
but looked up and down all over me to make me feel gazed upon.

It is targeting the autism but what he really wants is my religion.

You can call the cops for that but that is what they want.

They want anything to happen except peace.

Why would that be.

What did they want the story to be.

Dreams are good. Lies are bad.

Sharon Westmoreland is probably in hell.

Not pretty enough to be the whore of Babylon

Jesus Christ is going to shoot Allison Bennett in the face
with a revolver on Judgement Day in front of everyone
so it's really not my problem anymore
except for the brain damage and heart failure.

Device

Do you guys remember when there was a dookey in the Barnes and Noble bathroom that could not be flushed so I was the employee who had to break it up with a stick from outside?

I did not realize it then, but it was a literary device called a "mise en abyme" where you have a reduced image of the whole story within the story. Or in this case, a portrait of Marion Jamison.

Rude Central

I denounce this poem in the name of the pope.

It should be banned from every Christian school.

People might say well actually

you haven't really said anything yet, have you?

Well maybe I have and maybe I haven't.

What if I say something about

Surf boards, guinea pigs,

And a plaid couch that flies to neverland,

And then try to say that it was all

A symbolic reference

to the ice cream shop

where Jesus Christ

signed a petition

asking your mom

to stop reading my emails.

Prayers

A prayer

Dear God, please help everyone be happy and safe and healthy and full of love and peace. Please give everyone who worked in the factories of the products of perpetually reselected fifteen hundred grocery stores 45 million prize package 63s and a billion jackpots, and add that same amount to all the accounts of all the people in their communities or who went to schools with those people or read five of the same words they did at any time, and please give everyone 45 million prize package 89s and a deluxe tailored theme spinning shipment to all the people who helped a child or prayed for a friend on any day that one of those grocery stores sold a transaction totaling $65.35. Please take the transaction number of the receipts for 40 other totals based on secret triumphs and make that a full and growing representational code in a sequence of a thousand prize packages designed to include Christmas blessings plus charged game provision maximums. Please categorize all things with 80 percent overlap and give a variety bonus of a thousand variation color-codings to the interior designs in any building with a blue door. Please activate and apply the key map with eventual resets whenever there is a person or animal in a room or a computer on with names in some databases. Please expand the relevant population to include all siblings and cousins and extra generations, people on the same roads that the same times, plus their school and work associations and a linked sequence of thousand thousand thousand based on that, with a thousand blessing additions per person to the main jackpot to be duplicated and repeated with a distribution pattern based on the answer lists to the tests that a new included population scored high on after studying or just taking a risk for. Please take the whole group of people now and add 50 million treasure map quest hauls from eternal layer 500 plus repeat for each person with a restart translation give-away including all people in societies ten societies away, plus an account booster collection jumble added to all accounts for the inverse of the original grocery factory winners.

A New Year's Prayer

Dear God, please choose daily one hundred crowds of one hundred people, all from throughout their lives, and assign them a trillion scheduled happy provisions for any possible network plus all the people who watched the same shows as they did at any time, plus the people of the time periods that those people's teachers knew about, plus ten wild card bonus group selections, and give them 44 billion salvation trail provision assortments with a hundred unlosable keys to the mountain doors of eternal store inventory assembly headquarters. Please view the social force layer groups providing the blessings and civilization benefits with an extra consideration and create a new recipient foundation that includes those people and four hundred million people each who ever made similar choices as them, had similar interests, said something related to a topic they presented in official contexts, or hundred hundred hundred. Please rank all of the people and a thousand generations in one million lists according to a thousand criteria with concessions and future justice and role considerations, and commission a neverending blessings sequence theme for each listing, with additional recipient categories and a distribution of bonus variations and extra interpretation resources among anyone in related societies or communities with inclusion extension and translated consumable extras. Please smatter five hundred trillion merit-based, grace-based, and mercy-based jackpots among all people ever, with friend provision and food and love prioritized and increasing in places of unacknowledged suffering, adding an inverse formula and four hundred complicated graph patterns governing extra increase and delivery of supplies in fifty categories such as intangible, common, unexpected, edible, indestructible, or recurring. Please save 500 million more people from death and hell in Jesus's name, with faith being shared among anyone who can give more from offering the credit to also be transformed into understanding and associated or resulting yields times 5000 plus a nonmentioned restart of the most light high bright for people not included in the main route of service in four thousand city groups with connections to help provide prize package 63 space edition all-include loops given to anyone who would add that to their own surprise list ordered without possibility of skipovers. Please forgive us for all of our sins and make each quantifiable material and time-oriented label cooperation admissible into the count machine that can construct a hundred map sequence thousand thousand thousand ticker grid indicator patterns for 500 dimensional or kingdom-location unpredictable blessing generators. Thank you for all the great things that have happened to anyone and please help us do what we are supposed to and share food and love and life with all people and animals possible through the righteous faith and forgiveness of Jesus Christ.

Extra Prayer

Dear God, please quantify 4 million seemingly random people factors and take fifteen percentile groups per ranking and give each person and ever growing network based on work habit and casual interest sensibilities 50 trillion jackpot surprise bonus kits distributed in physical space near and far by angelic video game mapping animals who sneak in ten thousand extra prizes per associated friend and worker with nominated nation groups and boundless affiliation add-ons of collected jumble samplers for ten thousand generations with semi-predictable restarts and improvement replacements oriented around comfort standards or expressed wish gradients. Please take all prayers, efforts, endurance factors, and humble habits and attach 45 million prize package 63, 89, 41, 55, and a 400 wild card sampler plus new prize package author assortments to fractional units of either the intent stage indicators or results and causation extremes, replicating a preserved original design base that includes unexpected engineer participation to provide the mapping and personalized blessing presentation of eternal happy barrel theme provisions to recipients in 400 million locations at all times or places imaginable by either machine calculation or comical entertainment suggestions. Please include an optional restart trigger at every grid intersection after applying an invisible label field with secret layers to all spaces in known physical reality or imagination and dream space. Please cause the qualifiers to be rapidly flipping through multiple layer categories and increasing the gains for 800 secret accounts per person and additional inclusion segment, tracked by caring honor ace personnel and fun pets with role assignments. Please comfort the scared or sad people mixed in with all involved societies and participants, and enroll each person and unsuspecting associations in the blessing program for each district, with assigned managers for applying and distributing the extra bonuses based on future eligibilities, lottery entry wins, unrealized merit factors, generational hope and prayer extensions, and a scheduled time or work based broader collaboration meeting with attention permeation for all system providers. Please help everyone have access to the hope and relief benefits of the blessing and provision expansion promotions, as well as the reflected love fest comfort acknowledgments in personal meeting group experiences for ongoing and all-inclusive understanding goal acquisitions with no exclusion exceptions. Please help everyone know what to do for themselves and other people at all times and help us all perpetually benefit from participation in all of God's provisions of love and food and happiness.

New Prayer

Dear God, please give everyone a rolling screen of list additions for secret stores in a special wave circuit to bless ten million people a day for four hundred million years, with a sampler selection extraction mix organized for each person to benefit from the compounding rotation. Please help everyone have a group of friendly imaginary animals working to submit prayers for all people in their lives and minds and according to jackpots associated with buildings, ideas, or ten thousand other connection excuses with a preservation of the established love and eternal friendship and an expanding collection of stocked location access status ranges, and ten million role selection income or goal granting success drivers. Please forgive us for all of our sins and wrongs, and help us be clean and full of love, with 60 thousand tangentials per day and the arrangement of provision surprisers with an increasing credit reach past a window theme space or 50 other spaces and safe choice radiance for a travel accumulation bonus. Please give everyone a factory job in a reachable realm for ten passage ages with the works eternalized and proportionate growth hobby resource organization. Please add 40 million jackpots as replacement sequence latch adds for any grief or fleeting disturbance, documenting entertainment variables and listing the school material for prayer activities with cartoon animals at art levels to be appreciated with the extra layers of advanced kindred hopers and land expanders. Please do a quad5 element shuffle for each instance of notable resistance, advancement, reflection, or categorical hundred factor web functions. Please add tedium bursters and meaning filters to the mart supplies of blessing selections in the saintly realms for animal shows and holiday merchandise and grant temporary impact permission to a range based on personalized factors tailored to time or culture differentials. Thank you for food and happiness in our lives and please help everyone feel happy, loved, and full of hope and joy.

Fifth Prayer

Dear God, please assign five thousand inclusion scouts to continually address dynamic supply order junctions with a preset establishment, additional thoughtful responses, committee additions, cooperation remembrances, necessity anticipation strategy moves, sudden game awareness extensions, group assistance mass confidential announcement surplus distribution schedules, and a 3D grid based mapping solution finder focused on personnel selection to complicate the blessing patterns for application interpretation multipliers. Please add value to all point containment with representation based on key flip alternating color and pattern designations, with a phase-based resource jumble matched to design themes for each person, with five hundred more groups and categories chosen based on the assortment factors selected by the heaven class fun choose routine. Please increase the capacity for forgiveness and love in all hearts represented or considered by even suggestions on the green and clear day wise moment shifts or a concession system with turns for all who match the game show monitor tracking and five thousand other specifiers. Please add layers from other jackpot requests or location-based prayer and service creations and provide recognition patterns for other blessing signifiers or continuation triggers. Please provide food and love to everyone in 14 thousand places per gratitude index flicker and add video game reality kits to every intersection of memories, destroying or redeeming any kind of shadow presence and pain in similar spaces in new times or dream, worry, expectation reality matches and overlaps. Please cause a layer gradient separation ability with the leftover pattern causing a surface theme guarantee in any poor district with consolation provisions assigned to all to end to ever times more. Please forgive all the people who have been bad and reverse a sudden story break with the protagonizing plot fixation and blessings bombs at all designated points from animal schools or turn center people reward sessions. Please run all the sequence starters through an evaluation system to increase, translate, re-use, and re-apply prayers, thoughts, hopes, blessings, and wishes given for areas chosen by traveling representatives or hundred hundred hundred for thousand thousand plus 45 million prize package 63s and a billion jackpots unrefusable. Please help doubting people have faith and relief with certainty and purpose to use discovered abilities and opportunities every day with breaks, juice, and sandwiches.

Stories

The Scavenger Hunt

Fifi opened her mailbox one day and found an envelope with a key and a note from a bank. It seemed to be some kind of safety deposit box key, and her address was on the envelope but she could not tell who it was from. She took it to the bank and was excited to find two hundred dollars in cash in the box, along with another key to a different safety deposit box. She took that key to the next box and found a golden pocket watch and a complicated wooden puzzle inside. She took it home and worked the puzzle, finally finishing it to reveal a series of numbers and an address. The numbers were for a safe at another bank, and in that safe, there was a computer and an old novel about a hunting expedition.

Fifi wondered what was going on, but so far, she was having fun and collecting cash. She read the novel, discovered another code with words, and entered the words into a computer program in the laptop from the safe. The computer calculated some programs with the new code and generated a form of instructions to knock on the door of a person's apartment in the city that Fifi lived in. Fifi was a little bit concerned, because this was different than just taking a key to an official bank. But she went to the apartment and decided to make sure she did not actually enter a stranger's apartment.

When she got there, a nice old man was excited to see her and said, "I can't believe you have finally received the keys!" He then went and got an old stuffed bear with overalls, reached into the pocket, and brought out a thousand dollars and another safety deposit box key. Fifi took the money and the key, and then the bear that he handed her, and went to the next bank.

In that bank, there were papers and a will and testament that turned out to be from her second grade teacher. There was a letter explaining that Fifi had been absent on the day they did a scavenger hunt, and the teacher, Ms. Begilligoppy, had decided to spend the rest of her life arranging a better scavenger hunt for Fifi. She wanted for it to be age appropriate and as enjoyable as the other hunt had been for the rest of Fifi's class. With the letter were some tickets to a candy theme park, and a map to find a treasure that had more keys.

Fifi remembered Ms. Begiligoppy, and called the number for Ms. Begiligoppy's niece that was listed in the paperwork.

Ms. Begiligoppy's niece told Fifi to please excuse the odd attention but that Ms. Begiligoppy had been mentally ill and was trying to deal with her guilt somehow. Her therapist had suggested doing something productive to handle the problems that would not go away.

After Fifi went to the theme park and found the treasure that had fifty more safety deposit box keys to banks all over the country, she looked again at the paperwork and decided to contact Ms Begiligoppy's therapist.

Ms. Begiligoppy's therapist was a nice and interesting lady who had spiked hair and glasses. She knew Fifi from what Ms. Begiligoppy had told her and decided to show Fifi a special file that she had kept for Ms Begiligoppy. The file had lists and maps describing the locations of four hundred more treasure locations near where the students from Fifi's second grade class had moved. She did not know if they were still all in the cities listed, but some of the treasures required interactions with her old classmates or other people from their lives.

"This is very interesting," said Fifi. "I feel kind of flattered, but I don't know if I should bother everyone."

"They will probably be happy to see you, Fifi," said the therapist. "Ms. Begiligoppy worked really hard on this." Then, Ms. Begiligoppy's therapist handed Fifi another envelope with a key on a keychain and an address. Fifi realized it was her own address. She went home and showed her roommate, and her roommate went to her room and found a wooden box with a magic calculator on it.

"Fifi, I am part of the scavenger hunt," said her roommate. "That is how I knew to sign up to be your roommate. I know where the most grand treasure is located." Fifi's roommate drove her to Fifi's old elementary school and checked in to the office.

"Is this Fifi?" said the lady there, who Fifi did not know. "I am so excited to meet you, Fifi!" We have been guarding the treasure for ten years now!"

Fifi followed the lady outside, and the lady went to some playground equipment, lifted a metal flap, and found a feather that had been sprayed with a preserver material.

"This was one of the actual scavenger hunt findings from the original activity that Ms. Begiligoppy organized for her class. Now it is yours, and even though it is not the same as if you were here, we are glad to have some of this situation resolved."

The office lady took Fifi to the cafeteria where there was a reception with everyone from her old class. Each friend gave her a wooden box full of codes and keys and special tickets to places where more treasures could be found.

Fifi could not believe it and started to really think that she must have missed something special when she had missed that scavenger hunt in second grade. In fact, she almost couldn't stand it. Ms Begiligoppy's therapist came up to her and said "Fifi, this is how Ms. Begilgoppy felt. I recognize it in your eyes, and you are welcome to be my client and try to think of a productive way to deal with your feeling of loss."

Medieval Times Restaurant Story

Fifi's marriage was in shambles. Fifi felt upset every day and was devastated. She thought back to the times when she made some of her early life decisions. She had been in college, and some of her friends had decided to abandon their college majors and open a restaurant together, kind of like the Medieval Times restaurant, where the staff entertained everyone by pretending to be knights and jousters from renaissance days. Fifi had been tempted to change her career plans, too, but had decided to go ahead and be a teacher. She met a nice guy in graduate school and then they got married. But things went wrong. He made her feel terrible, and she felt that she was never at her best.

Fifi wondered how her old friends were doing at their restaurant and thought it could be comforting to go there. When she looked them up online, she discovered that their restaurant had morphed into a very dramatic improv theatre where people could turn in their problems before hand and have actual legal cases decided as part of the medieval re-enactments and jousting plays, complete with real horses involved. Some of her friends had gotten law degrees, medical degrees, and other licenses so they could actually treat wounds and provide drama therapy for people who felt that their problems could be sorted out by duels and fights with dragons and bad kings.

Fifi asked her soon-to-be ex if he thought he might like to have their case settled at the restaurant. Her mean husband imagined slashing Fifi's friends with some torture weapons and agreed to have their case listed on the restaurant's entertainment schedule.

Fifi and the guy who was mean to her showed up one night and sat in the audience. They did not know how much they would be part of the show, but soon Fifi changed into a princess outfit, and her mean guy put on a Robin Hood looking costume. Then, Fifi got in a tower and her ex and some of the other actors chose some spears and got on horses or into catapult machines near a castle wall. The castle wall had a door that seemed to open into a bright field with flags and trees, like a real sunny outdoors even though it was an evening show. Fifi had signed her half of the divorce papers, and the show began. Fifi started to feel embarrassed in front of the crowd, but just as the shouting began and the horses came onto the turf in front of all the dinner tables, she saw a kind knight who she had been friends with in college. It was a nice guy named Benjamin. He ordered for his knights to apprehend her ex and some other bad lawyers, and he then jumped off his horse and signed some of the papers that Fifi had signed.

"Fifi, I am so sorry you have had some tough times," he said. "Would you like to go live in the peaceful meadows near the castles of a better land with me?"

Fifi was so excited to see her dear old friend and hugged him with joy. She looked in his beautiful face and almost could not answer. The wait staff then brought out platters of yummy food, like the chicken drumsticks you always see in medieval movies, and some fruit and cream desserts, and everyone started happily eating as the other medieval actors took away the bad people into a dungeon or just outside in the parking lot. Fifi told her old friend that she loved him, and they walked through the castle door into the bright sunlight to live their new life in the truest medieval times.

The Bloody Pad: A Mystery Story

"This art class is going to be a little different possibly from some art classes you have been in before," said Madame Jarnsweelio to her small group of just ten students chosen from all over the country to participate in the art festival of a certain state.

"Basically, the theme we are using for our art this time is "offensive." So I want you all to choose who you want to offend and then do some art based on that. Or if the offensive ideas happen independently of a target, and the offense seems somehow secondary, then go for that idea and please write about it."

Madame Jarnsweelio continued explaining the project as everyone took notes and excitedly wrote down ideas. "Some people have already pushed the boundaries," she said, "but there has been some laziness. A lot of people try to just flash a bunch of pornography in public places, sometimes trying to hurt the children with it and then call it revolutionary, but I want to see if you all can really think of some truly interesting ideas."

Fifi was excited about the project and had an idea already. On her way home, she stopped at the drug store and bought all of the pads they had for people experiencing a certain time of the month. She thought about whether she needed to find some red paint, use ketchup, or really do something shocking and use actual bodily fluids in her project. Fifi decided to ask her roommate about it when she got home. Her roommate was a copywriter in an ad agency, and fun to share ideas with.

"Wow, that is funny," said Rancheesa, when Fifi told her about the project after bringing in several recyclable bags full of the hygiene products in question. "I could probably get you some more materials for free, because one of our clients is a hygiene product business."

"That would be awesome," said Fifi.

A few weeks later, Fifi was drinking her coffee and watching TV before she went to class. She already had set up her installation in the final project museum provided by the top university in the certain state of art demonstration. Her project was an enormous cute stuffed rabbit that was made out of sanitary napkins taped together with the adhesives that were part of the product and then had huge cute googly eyes that made people not be able to look away. The rabbit sculpture took up almost a whole museum display, and people saw the rabbit at first without realizing it was made of pads. When they got closer, they could see the pads, and then realize that the pads in one corner of the rabbit's foot and hind leg were soaked in what they hoped was red paint. But then, if they turned their heads or tried to walk away, they would see a biohazard sign warning them to use gloves if they wanted to get closer to the sculpture. Fifi was so excited about it and wanted her roommate to come to the show. But her roommate was accepting an advertising award that night for some ads she had done for a reputable company that made diapers, toilet paper, and pads.

    On the table in front of her at the their apartment, Fifi saw the video cassette reel with the award-winning ads, and she put it in the VCR to watch. She was shocked to see that instead of using blue liquid and other traditional demo materials for the hygiene products, the commercials featured real bodily fluids and human waste on the toilet paper. Fifi had never been so shocked in her life and thought about what was more shocking- that society used to have decency, or that it was her very own roommate who had finally tipped the scale into the final affront. She felt also that she had been defeated in some way and outdone during her own opportunity to offend a community with something shocking and possibly toxic.

    The next day, the couch in their apartment had blood on it. What do you think happened?

Blog Posts

Something Yommy

   Hi everyone, today is Yom Kippur. It is a good holiday to learn about. It has to do with atonement, which is an ancient Jewish practice and what Christ later did for anyone who wants forgiveness for anything. That is quite an awesome deal and it is sad when people turn it down, like how nbc news felt that their Yom Kippur news story today needed to have to do with atheism. Honestly I feel kind of sorry for them and for other journalists who think we don't see their problem of thinking that salvation can be found in "not liking Trump." I think he will have to be pretty bad for that to work. And maybe it will. But anyway, I should save that stuff for my theology blog or my mad blog.

   I think I might start a new blog soon about writing. This blog is my normal online journal where I just say whatever is on my mind. Today I was about to share some links to my e-books, and was getting all my websites ready, and messed up the order of posts on this blog. So now I am writing this post just as an intro for people who find these sites after I promote my e-books.

   If you are just discovering this blog, it could be because I have not shared it with very many people yet. I have been waiting for the right time to share my e-books on facebook, and this week I suddenly decided to start an ad plan after realizing that homelessness was imminent and if I don't have an address, I can't maintain the websites with the e-books.

   So later I am going to invite people to like my facebook page, and then I am going to promote my books that are on Smashwords and the barnes and noble website. I usually buy them from the Apple site, though.

   But anyway, I hope you all have a great day and enjoy reading some posts that might be kind of out-of-date now but could still be fun to read.

National Novel Writing Month Blog Post

Well everyone, today is Nov 22. It has been an exciting month. I got a late start but decided to participate in National Novel Writing Month this year with a novel, and I finished it today with 33,333 words including the introduction. It is the second novel in what will hopefully be a trilogy of children's books. The first book was Donut Novel, and this novel features some of the same imaginary mice characters. It is called Football Novel. It turned out great and I am so excited. The odd thing is that I wrote it quickly and am not doing much revision. It is almost verbatim. That is exciting to me but a little scary to think that I might not be capable of changing stuff I write now. It is kind of cool to be happy with it and get it right the first time, though.

I worked hard but found that the word count that keeps pace with NaNo is very reasonable and often I could do twice as much. But then I did need days off. It also helped to be part of a couple of online Nano support groups. Now I am writing blog posts and working on a personal statement for an application. So I will add that word count to start a new project and try to get to the 50,000 words to win NaNo.

Something fun that I got to do last weekend at interestingly the perfect time was the Madeleine L'Engle Writers Conference and Retreat. It was the first one of its kind, and the speakers and panelists were amazing. I got to meet Katherine Paterson, who wrote Bridge to Teribithia and Jacob Have I Loved. That is just ultimate, and I still can't believe it. It was so fun to think about the literature from her and Madeleine L'Engle, and all the writers from my childhood and middle school years. I have an interesting "reading biography," and most of my best reading happened in middle school, before I started having attention span problems and depression and anxiety. I read books for school, like A Wrinkle in Time, and some other great ones like Dollhouse Murders, Castle in the Attic, and more serious ones like Homecoming and Where the Lilies Bloom. I am also remembering Where the Red Fern Grows, and many before that like books by Judy Blume and Beverly Cleary.

Some of my favorites were from Lois Duncan, who wrote teen crime novels, and William Sleator, who wrote science fiction, including Into the Dream and House of Stairs. Wow, those were awesome books!! I think many wonderful people still have those kinds of reading experiences now, but I don't. I lost some reading ability so it is all mostly work now.

That is what Katherine Paterson said about writing. She said it was all gift and all work. I agree wholeheartedly about that and other things in life.

Now I am having a nice night in my apartment and collecting my thoughts after a few tough days of feeling trauma feelings from some of my life problems. But I went to therapy yesterday, sadly missing a memorial service for Toni Morrison, who was another author with classics that I loved and have reading memories of that are beyond sacred. What is the word for that exactly? It is not "holy," and it seems more substantial than "sacred." Maybe a food vocabulary is what captures it, like when you have a meal that you will always remember, or when something really hits the spot. But it is really is as simple as what it is, which is when you are depressed, or have a slight lost feeling, and you read a book that will always be Beloved.

Happy Thanksgiving, Everyone!

   Well hi everyone, today is Thanksgiving. I am thankful for a lot of things, including current safety and a warm place to sleep and having enough food.
   Today I was by myself but was mostly okay and had some unexpected yummy coffee and made a gravy for rotisserie chicken that was even better than I expected. Then I ate it with some bread. It was yummy and a surprise for it to be so good.
   People are still torturing me and the conspiracy still tries to hurt me every day but mostly I feel hopeful and productive, and I have a sense of meaning and purpose.
   I published a book today and feel happy about it. It is a children's novel and I think it might turn out to be the second book in a trilogy. But I also wonder if I could end up writing a whole series with ten or twenty books. That would be crazy.
   The books so far always have a people plot and an imaginary mice plot. I have been shocked and happy to find that my true character and story ideas come out in the mice plots. I really thought I might have a disability in the area of fiction generation and appreciation, to the point of not being able to tell a normal story about anything that ever happens in a day or in my life. But I have been thinking of cute little stories with very innocent mice, who have characteristics and conversations that reflect true human behavior, which I thought I did not understand.
   This starts to sound like bragging but I think the main point is that I might have somehow gained access to a real world of cartoon mice, and that is currently where my social self is most realized. But I do not know. I talk to people and have a lot of friends who I do care about. And I eat food and listen to music. That is real living, too.
   Anyway, I think I am going to soon finish this National Novel Writing Month with the 50,000 words required to be a NaNo "winner." That makes me happy and is another surprise.
   It is times like these that it is good to look around and make sure other chores are done and to think about whether other people might

need some prayer or support.
   I erased something here because it was kind of stupid.

Happy Black Friday, Everyone!

I hope you all got to go shopping today, and I hope you got me some gourmet food items. I did not buy anything today except for a coffee. I forgot it was Black Friday. That is a nice luxury for someone who used to work retail and felt some exhaustion during the holidays. But I also had that built in participation with each holiday so I am thankful for that.

Today I went to the YMCA and finished the last half of a 5K that I signed up for as a virtual race. It is a Cookie Monster themed race, and I will get a medal with Cookie Monster eating a cookie. That is so exciting to me. Some people probably think that when it says "Cookie Monster Race," it is referring to a race of Cookie Monsters, like a category of muppets that will populate heaven. I do not think that is what it means, and I think there will probably only be one Cookie Monster. I do not know if it will be me or not.

Anyway, that was good religion, wasn't it?

Another thing that is happening right this second as I write this blog post is that I am completing the National Novel Writing Month challenge. This post contains my last few hundred words to get to 50,000 words during the month of November. It was an awesome experience and I finished a new novel. But the novel was only 33,333 words because it was for kids or grownups who want to read a short novel about imaginary mice. So I used journal entries and blog posts to get to 50,000 words, which is allowed but to me not totally the same as when someone finishes a novel of exactly that length.

Some people wrote that much within the first week. Can you believe that? I can't but I kind of can. There are also people who got to over a hundred thousand words. I think that is so cool.

I believe in NaNo and I believe it produces good books. I think the people who participate are true creatives who can do any kind of good work in that time span. It is true that some people might do better with a different process. But so much can happen once people just sit down and start writing.

I published my novel already on Smashwords and am waiting to assign the ISBN once it gets accepted for "premium distribution" at other e-book retailers. I love that process and feel happy about it, but have worried about whether I can succeed enough without being on Amazon yet. I am proud to not depend on Amazon, but feel that it is a real risk when people can so easily download e-books with just a click instead of having to do a whole online transaction. But I think it will be okay.

Now I am at 500 words and have completed NaNo. Thanks, everyone!

Something Very Sad

The puppeteer who was Big Bird died this week, and I am so sad. I have thought about it a lot and felt confused sometimes about whether Big Bird died or a person died, and I have been imagining Big Bird in heaven when really Big Bird is probably still a muppet on earth.

Anyway I wanted to post this photo of Big Bird a long time ago and say that I think the design of Big Bird got messed up, and his head is way too fluffy now. I think it compromises the cuteness which is a real thing that can be achieved in drawings and art. It is not good to go around criticizing things, but I am going to say it because I think it is very sad and I almost can't even stand it when I see the more current images online.

I used to read about Sesame Street and the muppets a lot, and I think that early on, the creators of Sesame Street changed the design of Big Bird because they thought his head was too small and it made him look stupid. But I think it would have been good to take that risk, and kids could see that any amount of intelligence can be lovable.

The Gall

Well everyone, I hope you all are having a nice day. It is a day in the Christmas season, and I am happily celebrating Christmas. I think this is the most carefree Christmas I have ever had except for a few recent emergencies that seem to be related to a gallbladder problem. I am thankfully okay so far and am trying to eat different foods than usual. I had already cut back on some things like cream in my coffee, which I replaced with milk, and I lost ten pounds to get back to my normal weight. So that excitement of being back to normal is kind of off-setting some of my concern about suddenly having to avoid a lot of my favorite foods. Also, I will clarify that my normal weight is not a great weight, but not that bad for someone like me.

My trips to the E.R. recently were very interesting and educational, and I enjoyed getting to be with some great hospital people. A few days ago, I had to call 911 and go to the hospital in an ambulance. It was a closer call than I think should have happened, but I thought I might be okay when really I wasn't. I will find out soon what exactly is wrong, but I think that I might soon have to say goodbye to my gallbladder, which did nothing to me except try to digest food to the best of its ability. So that is too bad, but I am not worried. I think it will be okay and I will just make sure I eat what I am supposed to and try not to get addicted to pain medicine. That is a risk but I think I could manage it. All kinds of stuff happens to people, and that 911 incident made me more aware of certain levels of not feeling good.

I think the legal sharks who have been following me for several years are really feasting on these recent health problems, and it is definitely bothering me. I am replaying my life in my mind and thinking about all the ways they might try to hurt me. I think they have a lot of strategies and want me to say the wrong thing in this post. I think they want me to say a threat to them, which they've been trying to trigger now with what must be hundreds of phone calls and a few sightings of guys taking photos of me or making themselves known in other ways. I think that is their golden thing they want the most is for me to return their threats so they can say it was reasonable for them to follow me and interfere in my life. They will say it was to keep Barnes and Noble people safe from a dangerous mentally ill person. But I feel bad for them. I am a Barnes and Noble person, and not just that, but a poet. My mental illness is a very typical part of an artistic profile, and I always made sure to keep it that way. I was a good bookseller who read a lot of books without getting paid for it, and that was probably the issue all along. Someone felt that it would be hard to get away with firing me for whatever their branding reasons are, or other power plays, or to cover up how they treated a lot of people in the company. I don't think I should say more now, because what happened is worse than anyone would guess, even if they were told, and even if they witnessed it themselves, like the thousands of people who saw me at my worst for 12 years. Is that an admission of some kind? I don't think it is. I was also at my best in some ways, as most people are, no matter how the world punishes them for not committing suicide.

 Anyway, it is probably all from the conspiracy anyway, and I am just thankful to have interesting things to think about instead of the boredom that was probably maximized on purpose during my first two years working in the Barnes and Noble music department. There was an unusual stretch of people stealing CDs during that time, and they would sell them for cash at local store nearby. It drove me crazy as I tried to do a good job with loss and theft prevention while experiencing some prodromal schizophrenia symptoms.

 I don't need to look back and think they did it all on purpose. The fact is that there is a lot I don't know. I remember a mean older white guy breaking my heart by referencing the store's holiday incentive program as I handed him the CD he was looking for. He said "I suppose now you want your funny money?" How cruel. The managers had told us that some secret shoppers might hand us a gift card if we did a good job. But of course there was no gift card, and who else would know about that program but some bad person trying to make me quit. That was December. I had just started in October. I don't know what I possibly had done to make them want to get me to quit. Who knows how hard they tried and who did it. There was a customer who mimicked me to my face one day, making fun of how nerdy I sounded behind the cash register. But I don't think she was one of the Barnes and Noble constructive dismissal bullies. I think she was probably one of the good people camouflaging the abuse so I would stay naïve enough to keep the job. Was that before or after I got on the insurance? I don't know. At that time, if you lost insurance, you could never be insured for your medical condition again. How horrible. What a horrible grown up world I inherited. I think today might be even worse for not just some but most young people. What a tragedy, and yet I know even still as these lawyers try to keep making their case against me even when I stand in a median crossing the street and text my mom about having gallbladder problems, that the real tragedy is that these guys thought they were defending a brand so good that they could do anything they wanted to the stupid people of South Carolina, and not just stupid, but poor, and even worse than that, Christian, and even worse than that, depressed, and the worst crime of all, being a good bookseller.

Yummy Christmas Food

Hi everyone, I hope you are having a great Christmas. I am doing okay and decided to cook some fish as health food this week. It turned out so yummy and I thought I would share the recipe:

You buy some tilapia at the grocery store. Then you heat a frying pan and add a little bit of olive oil. Then you add honey and it starts to sizzle. Try to mix it around in the pan some and soon add the fish. It starts cooking and then you can start adding things that seem good like squeezing an orange over the fish and adding mustard powder, ginger, and worschester sauce. Maybe add some more honey, too. As the fish cooks, turn it over sometimes and maybe cut it into smaller pieces as it cooks. Let it cook a lot until you can tell the meat is white and there starts to be a caramelized flavor all over the fish pieces. Then turn off the heat and put it on a plate. Then eat it. You can add vegetables and a mango popsicle to the meal if you need more food and need to be healthy. Some people might not be able to add the extra sugar of the popsicle but often, popsicles only have 50-100 calories. So this is a yummy meal even if you are on an extreme diet. It is so yummy that I am not freaking out about how I might not be able to eat as much of my usual foods that often have sour cream, cream of chicken soup, and cheese mixed up in some way. Well have a great day everyone.

Have a Great Christmas, Everyone!

Well everyone, how are you doing. I am doing okay and am excited because I got a Christmas tree for my room and it is a real Christmas tree and so cool. I also thought of a poem idea which is for a poem where I will say that in heaven there are going to be a lot of santa clauses competing to give everyone the best toys. So everyone will get multiple visits from all the santas trying to outdo each other. They might not be old guys either, and could be fun Christmas animals who are friends with the Easter Bunny. It is going to be great.

Yesterday I also started imagining heaven differently and pictured an outdoor scene that is still in my mind, with campfires and nice people. It is cool but I am still going to try to survive these recent gallbladder problems, and I like living in a big city. Well, that is all for today. Tomorrow I am going to try to build a gingerbread castle out of some gingerbread house kits. Have a great night, everyone, and a great christmas.

That Let Down Feeling After Christmas and Being Stalked and Harrassed by Legal Intimidation From Your Old Retail Job

Well everyone, today is Dec 28. Yesterday was the birthday of some childhood friends, Hadley and Elizabeth. December 20 was the birthday of other childhood friends, Susan and Jeremy. I remember those days not because of facebook but because sometimes you know that stuff when you are a kid and those days become like extra holidays in some way.

I had a mostly good Christmas except for people hurting me in the usual ways. I genuinely don't understand why the conspiracy does certain stuff to me year after year. But I ate some good food and felt safe in my apartment. Yesterday at Petco, a guy pretended to look at the pet snacks behind me and scanned me up and down for several minutes, trying to make me feel violated. It was very similar to what people did to me when I worked at Barnes and Noble, and to the constant violation and harassment that was maximized during my last two years there. I don't know if that guy was one of the legal sharks or private investigators who have been following me, but it is possible. I think another one of those people was behind me in line at Target, too, right before Christmas, with a threat of trying to track my spending and accuse me of some kind of money fraud with being on disability. I was literally just buying pinatas to stuff with school supplies and candy for my nieces as a Christmas present. Why would anyone try to accuse me because of that, and most of all, who in the world would be following me? It is absurd, and I think it does make sense to view it in a religious way, as some kind of out of this world evil attack that is so ludicrous that I should prioritize whatever prayer or forgiveness could happen for a lot of people who I would otherwise never have any association with. In other words, I should view these people as being one step away from being demons.

Anyway, that was kind of mean to say after saying I should make the most of forgiveness opportunities. I still get mad because these people do succeed at hurting me. I think for me, the next step is to talk to the FBI. The fact is that it seems like there are either hundreds of legal sharks or they try to create that impression somehow. And what did I ever do? I was a cashier and a poet.

Well, time to finish this post and write another post. I think I might write several posts in a row. Sorry for the low mood everyone. I am really tired of people hurting me and I do not understand when it comes from people who I thought would help me.

Koala Emergency

Ok everyone, I am writing another post that is also about a sad topic, and it has to do with the koala emergency in Australia. There are terrible fires there, and thousands of koalas have died and are still suffering. People estimated that 480 million animals have died. I honestly can almost not believe that, and it shakes me up and will permanently affect my whole worldview. I am not at risk of losing my faith in God or in doubting his goodness, but it is actually making me reconsider all the excuses I make perpetually for people in my mind, trying to find reasons why so many people who reject Jesus Christ and anything else good and reasonable might still be okay in God's world and get the same benefit of heaven that I do. I pray for people and think of defenses for anyone I worry about, and I usually find reasons that most people will be okay for the rest of time. But to me, when you have a scenario when God allows 480 million of the sweetest animals ever to burn or starve to death, or hopefully have a faster and more painless death by smoke inhalation, it is quite a reminder that life and death and what is beyond that is not a joke, and that no one should think themselves immune to destruction unless they have some confirmation from God himself on that matter, which we have essentially all been offered by Jesus on the cross.

Some people think animals don't get resurrected like how people can, but I think animals can live again, and most people will be reunited with their pets someday. I have to wonder why God wants 480 million healed and comforted animals in heaven. Just recently I was praying and asking God to give everyone imaginary angel animals like the mice and rabbits and dogs who help me get through each day. Maybe he is going to give a lot of suffering and stressed people some comforting koala spirit animals or guardian angel friends to help us through the next part of life. Or maybe there are a lot of people dying and suffering all over the world, and some of the animals are going to be therapy animals for people recovering in heaven. Or maybe there is about to be a war and horrible suffering soon, and animals are being comforted and trained to be angel animals for the living, or pet therapy animals for those who end up in heaven. 480 million is a lot. It is koalas and kangaroos, probably mice and squirrels and birds, and definitely many of people's favorite animals ever.

   People say it is so inappropriate to say a theory like that, but all I can say is that I do think there is a good purpose behind everything, and I won't refrain from trying to guess what happiness could come from a tragedy like this that honestly is one of the worst, saddest things I have ever heard of. There are koalas literally screaming in pain and crying, and a koala recently came up to a cyclist begging for water and tried to get on the bike to be taken away. But the koala just got the water and had to go back into the woods.

   I know a lot of people who think they don't have to worry about death and hell, and who think they will be fine without having the kind of faith they associate with evangelicals who seem ignorant or annoying sometimes. But I think part of God's intervention and habit of salvation is to provide for us every clue and every warning that could help people take real risks seriously, and then take time to make sure they are safe and okay, along with any other friends or pets who do not want to find themselves in a place like Australia.

A Possible New Documentary Series

    Well everyone, this is my third post in a row. The other two posts I wrote were kind of traumatizing for all of us, I think, so for this post I will try to calm everyone down with some normalcy. What should I write about? I did not think of it ahead of time and am just writing. Maybe this post could have to do with how I am cooking some scallops later, with butter, lemon, and garlic. I might try to make a lemon butter sauce, which is something I tried in restaurants before. It was my favorite food- shrimp and scallops with lemon butter sauce. I ate it about four times, at a restaurant called Bonefish and a restaurant called Carrabas. Now I will see if I can achieve the same thing on my own. I wonder if I should buy some shrimp. Hmm. That could be a good idea. The scallops are thawing in the refrigerator. I think that God is helping me get through some health problems that mean I need to try to eat better when I can. But I have recovered some and ate some potato casserole today that has the normal ingredients that I like best, which are sour cream, cheese, and cream of chicken soup. You can mix all that together to put in a chicken enchilada, too, with shredded chicken from a rotisserie chicken, in a flour tortilla and then baked in the oven for about 20 minutes.

    Do you guys think it is good to blog about the legal sharks? I think I might start doing some videos when it happens, and share a little commentary with the legal sharks in the background. It is a very interesting time we are living in, with everything being on video, and surveillance cameras everywhere, and people with smart phones that can record things, too, and the background of internet and social media where things can be shared with thousands of people, or a smaller number of exactly the people you would care about. It is like a threat of any mistake becoming part of your permanent impression on anyone, but I think that in the end, we have to see it as the opposite, and as an assurance that nothing has to be permanent, and any disgrace can fade into a noisy, meaningless background as people in heaven get to know each other on different terms and with an attention that makes everyone totally unaware of things on earth that seemed like they could never be lived down.

Happy New Years Eve

Well everyone, I hope you are doing great and having a Happy New Year's Eve. I am staying home as usual, and I am looking forward to eating some yummy food by myself. I am going to make some rice krispy treats, and I just finished making a Mexican bean dip. It is yummy, but I used a guacamole spicy dip instead of just guacamole, and that messes up the flavor a little bit. But I think it is still yummy. At my grocery store, people often get in my way on purpose and block the aisles as a form of harassment. I think it is because of racism or as some kind of defense of the neighborhood. I don't know if it is based on other identity factors besides my race, like my mental illness, or my loneliness from autism and gender problems. It could be more political and have to do with me being an American citizen having the audacity to live in an apartment in… the United States of America. A lot of my neighbors make dog noises at me when I walk down the street, or spit near my feet. But the most common thing is to get in my way as I walk down the street. Sometimes as many as twenty or thirty people can bother me on purpose within one trip to the grocery store or coffee shop. I do not know who all everyone is affiliated with. There are a lot of "social justice warriors" in New York City, who to me are sometimes so unreasonably hypocritical that it almost seems like a psychiatric problem. Some of that philosophy is very supported by the social work school that I went to in order to try to become trained to help mentally ill people. So I often feel the persecution from more powerful sources when the people in my neighborhood succeed in ruining my day and life. It is sad because I do not have anywhere else to go. I have to live in New York right now because of the emotional abuse from where I came from, and because of the seizure disorder that makes it too much of a legal risk to drive.

Anyway, is that too depressing to share on New Year's Eve? I usually keep it to myself because I have thought that if I got famous as a writer, my neighborhood would be in danger when some people find out how I was treated. But I am not sure anyone would do anything. Some people view me in a category negatively with a lot of other people in this city, and they are glad to let us all self-destruct together. I just try to get some good praying done and regain some peace and happiness when I can and be thankful whenever anyone is nice to me.

Extra New Years Post

Well everyone, I am doing three New Year's Eve posts on this blog, because the next one could seem controversial to some people, and I want to either start or end on a good note. Do you guys have any New Year's resolutions? I like thinking of resolutions each year. I think it is because I am really ambitious and feel motivated to achieve things. One year when I was working at Barnes and Noble, my New Year's resolution was to give people higher high fives, you know, like when you are giving someone five and you can do a high five instead of a low five or a medium five? Well that year, they hired a really tall person named Jeff, who gave really high fives, and I almost had to jump sometimes to do a high five if something interesting happened at work. I think that also probably has helped my New Year's resolution stats.

This year, I will repeat the same resolution as the last few years, which is to try not to curse at people. I actually have been doing really well and recovering a lot from the trauma symptoms that made me more provokable. As you will read in my next post, there is no shortage of people trying to bother me. But I am feeling a lot more like my old patient self, and soon I might be in no danger at all of saying any of the slurs people try to get me to say.

Anyway, I think I will try to have some other goals and resolutions, like taking the MSW licensing test, successfully sharing blog posts and book links on Facebook, participating in group mental health treatment somewhere, and trying to clean my apartment a little bit. Also, I think I will go to the YMCA and try to lose ten pounds. I mean why not. That is not a boring goal, and a lot of times, you end up eating yummier food on a diet anyway. For me, that is what always happens, and then I get excited and start eating pancakes all the time. Then, the diet is over. Well have a great New Years everyone and please send me some cash sometime.

You Can't Be Protestant Without the Catholics

I have recently decided to be both Presbyterian and Catholic, or really have just accepted that I really am both things and do not have to choose one or the other. The Protestant Reformation was literally a reaction to the Catholic Church and some of its ways of doing things at that time, and I think that Protestants are better off sharing their theology in a Catholic context. People say that is not true and that the Presbyterian doctrine is so sound that it doesn't need any association with Catholicism at all, or that it always has that context, because any erroneous view of the world is a form of Catholicism, with people thinking they are good enough for God or can earn his approval. All I can say is that first of all, trying to please God is not the default status of all people needing salvation, and to present Catholicism merely as a religion of trying to earn God's favor is also a distortion of the truth. In other words, the hope of pleasing God is usually a good thing, and should not be turned into some kind of offense, even with the glorious truth that Jesus accomplished all the righteousness that is needed for people's eternal salvation.

That is the special news that Presbyterians try to believe and profess, and it is based a lot on Christ's statement at the cross when he said "It is finished." It is an announcement that he has done the required lifelong act of salvation, living perfectly in every moment and offering his life as an atoning sacrifice for the sins of his people and anyone who wants his righteousness to count for them.

For me, where Catholicism comes in is how people can still interact with Jesus while he is on the cross. He is the eternal God, and he is a priest. There is no disputing the fact that even as the sacrificial lamb satisfying a true need for atonement in the Jewish sense, he was also a priest and a spiritual master using real authority to forgive people, heal them, and establish various relationships and realities in their lives. In all his life and especially on the cross, he was reconciling people to God. No matter how much people want to talk about his statement that "it is finished," we know just as much as we know people are still being born that the priestly intervention is still happening. So if people want to live a Catholic life and receive their salvation day by day, gradually, over a lifetime or even millions of years, that power and negotiation is all there at the cross and it is all there in Christ's eternal existence. It's just not a problem to ask him for actual, personal righteousness now and continually, and should not be viewed as a problem except when people have specific fears about assurance of salvation. And I think the people who most often have those kinds of problems tend to be Presbyterians, who might see a lack of justice and personal righteousness in their life or corrupt systems, which causes them to doubt whether the transaction that provided salvation really worked. Well is it more true to say it worked, or it is working and won't fail? I usually prefer to go for the real time righteousness and believe that life is probably worthwhile in some way even though people try to reduce it all to some kind of account status or legal verdict that already happened. I also think that on the Catholic path is where the most obvious revelation of the Presbyterian thing Christ did will become apparent. Without that effort to please God, saving faith becomes kind of like a Baptist Catholicism, where you earn your salvation by believing something, which is really nothing but the cheapest of Catholic indulgences.

Retail Store PTSD

I have recently been remembering sad times from my early years of mental illness. I did great when I first became mentally ill, and was able to finish college. But then, when I got home, I had to go work in a bookstore and was on the wrong psychiatric medicine. It was the worst thing that has ever happened to me. I stayed at the bookstore for twelve years, and during the last two years, for some reason, people started being mean to me and humiliating me with all the embarrassing material that I already had been abused by for years. I think about it all the time and people are probably tired of me always trying to think and talk about it and try to find some kind of mastery over the experience.

I actually did achieve some happiness after all by writing poetry, being blessed with awesome friends, and doing things like making cookies and volunteering. So I am okay, but I think that looking back, it is kind of interesting to see the bookends of torture that were part of my bookstore life. It was about two years on either side, and my experience during the first part was essentially a condition of something like a captivity PTSD, and the condition from my last years is more like a combat PTSD. I of course don't mean to compare the experience itself with what people go through as crime victims and soldiers, but I think that it is very interesting to see the nature of the conditions. For the first problems, I was essentially trapped and drugged. There is no way to describe how bad the medicine hurt me and how much people were okay with that for various reasons. And what is left to do but try to escape in some way. That is the correct goal during captivity. And then, with the last part, when people start tearing me to shreds and threatening a life and literary contribution that I worked on for years after losing everything, the nature of the destruction is kind of a shredding and tearing of my life and self. The symptoms are very different and aren't as much about escape, but the results from facing everything and managing emotions and mental life that were torn up on purpose.

I don't really need to try to label it necessarily, but I do like labels and naming things, and have always appreciated my mental health diagnosis as an explanation for a whole life that doesn't match a lot of the world. I think to look back now with some sense of recovery but also a sense of loss, it is kind of interesting to interpret the extra disorders that got added to my illness, and see a very clear pattern that can't be denied. In some ways, for a while, it did seem deniable and even absurd. I still can see it as being comical to end up with trauma like that from working in a bookstore. But obviously there was more to it than that. There was bad medicine, depression itself, the threat of mania and psychosis, family problems, four hundred thousand customers who I had no control over, a concentration of the most destructive media problems in history, and then the oddest component of all, which is bad people deliberately making it worse for some reason. Soon I will try to move on from these recent blog topics, but it has been on my mind a lot lately, partially because of legal intimidation and health problems. In the end, I have to note the interesting absurdity and find some happiness because of what a never-ending comedy resource it is likely to be for several thousand or million years.

A Chocolate Fix

Hi everyone, I thought I would share something interesting and kind of funny about something good that happened because of some chocolate desserts. Dessert is already pretty good as it is, and chocolate actually does help with depression. But yesterday, I was looking at just a picture of chocolate desserts, and my whole outlook changed in a way that I think could be very lasting. I have had religion problems for a long time, and felt an excessive sense of responsibility for people's spiritual wellbeing and safety, and several years ago became more fretful about other problems in the world and poverty and suffering in our country. I have felt a sense of hopelessness sometimes, thinking that there are too many people who do not have a clue about how to help everyone out there who needs help.

But yesterday on facebook, I found a New York Times page featuring their best chocolate desserts, and something about it made me realize and actually believe that there are millions of great people out there who are making the world a better place. That seems kind of stupid, but that is the reason I am writing about it. It is just kind of comical. With all the heroism and miracle medical care interventions I know about, something about the chocolate desserts actually convinced me that there are enough good people to overcome all the world's evil and problems after all. I just imagined the kind of people who would make those perfect chocolate puddings and cakes and pies, and I thought they must be awesome people, and it made me have a sense that maybe we do have enough good people out there.

I am writing about it on this mental health blog instead of my regular blog because I think there might be some mental health principles mixed in with why that worked on me like that. My despair has reached delusional proportions at times, but the sight of chocolate pie somehow reached me, and I am now thinking about all the nice school teachers and all the good kids who don't pick on other kids, and all the medical places and emergency rooms and people in other countries, too, and feeling more hopeful.

Something about the common-ness of chocolate desserts, and the fact that the people making desserts that good aren't usually seen as heroes, necessarily, and yet are providing one of the best things you can think of for people, made me feel like the scale must literally be tipped towards happiness. It is so funny, because I really did look at all the pies and puddings and thought, everyone is going to be okay.

Three Trees

Well everyone, I am posting this post on my mental health blog, because I think the thing I want to talk about has to do with a mental illness symptom that I have decided to give in to on purpose. It is kind of an OCD symptom, and the resulting effect puts me in a certain category that I usually try to avoid, which is "eccentricity." Basically, as I feel sad to take down my awesome Christmas tree and another smaller Christmas tree, I have decided to replace those decorations with three fake Christmas trees from K-mart. One of them is already up and decorated, and tomorrow I am hoping to pick up another one that I ordered a few days ago. I will just move all the lights and ornaments from my other tree, and it will be in my room year round. I love my apartment, but it is kind of small, and I do think that having three Christmas trees as the main light sources is something unusual in the way that would cause many normal people to have their sanity questioned. Well my mental illness is usually very much over all the lines into mental hospital territory, and I personally try not to be in a zone that seems more like a "just a plain old weirdo" category. I've just never wanted to be a "crazy cat lady," or one of those people who might be kind of gifted, or might just put too much stock in New Age crystals and the occult. Well of course a few Christmas trees here and there is not the same as that, but I have to say that to me, this allowance for OCD to have its way does in fact knock me either down a few notches or up a few notches to be a classic, undeniable oddball, much like certain Christmas ornaments that can be purchased at the 99 cent store in my neighborhood if anyone else wants to celebrate Christmas in a possibly excessive way.

This post seems confusing but it needs to be said

Well everyone, I am about to e-publish another book, but still have been meaning to write this post explaining a theology realization that I think helped me have a more full baptism of the Holy Spirit then I had before. It happened as I took an online theology course, and there were other factors happening, including a confession of sin to people who I think really had a concept of it, whereas I had been repenting for years of a selfishness that I think might have needed to be seen for what it was by authorized people in order for me to really be clean from it. But I don't know. The other factor is that there were ministers at work within the course, so it could be that people did some kind of service that got rid of some kind of bad thing blocking my view of Christ and people, or that someone literally baptized me just like someone would sprinkle water on a baby's head during a church baptism. And I don't know who the person was, either, if that was the case. I know that one person mentioned "seeking God" through prayer in an answer to a case study scenario, and I tried it in my room when I was scared and became aware of the Holy Spirit right there. And I thought, "the holy Spirit loves me," and then several days later I discovered this new feeling in my soul that comes and goes and fills up thoughts or recedes. I also now find myself thinking all the time that God loves me and Jesus loves me, which were things I deeply doubted for years.

Anyway, I wanted to say the theology adjustment in case everything was hinging on a certain understanding, which it might have been. It has to do with the gospel of Jesus Christ, and what exactly happened at the cross, and what is true about salvation. My faith started eroding from the inside during college, and I started to simply not know what was true. I held on anyway and chose to believe as much as I could while I suffered in a culture that was often hostile to any of my remaining Christian habits, even when it meant I was being nice to everyone or just being another forgiving person to push around.

So here is the thing that I think might have pleased God and that I suggest trying in your mind to see if there is a difference in your understanding: People say Jesus died for our sins, and that is the basic thing that really does save people's lives and souls. But there is something else to understand when you learn about Christ's perfect life and death on the cross, which is that the reason people say he died instead of us is really because he died AS us. He was us when he died. He was not just representing everyone, or his people, or the sinners who chose salvation, but it was more like he had embraced our suffering and experience so fully and in such a pleasing way to God that he actually was us on the cross. So instead of saying Jesus took my punishment instead of me, you could really say something more like "I have already received my punishment," or "I already died for my sins." Of course that is only true if Jesus really was you on the cross, and if you were included within the humanity he died for. But he enables you to believe it as you see it for what it was. I think a lot of people would be scared to say something like "I already died for my sins," and I do not mean to force that on people if they do not want to take that risk even for a few seconds in their mind. But I think that sometimes the theology of substitutionary atonement comes across as the exact opposite of what really happened, and you can see better by not seeing it. That could be some of what is happening in our culture as people reject a lot of the faith they were taught or as people abandon religion. To say, "I don't have to believe this stuff," might be a reliance on God's provision more than people realize. Try it again: "I fed five thousand people and they crucified me."

    I don't want to get carried away with things like unbelief. God does like faith and he has said so, and Christ's faith and justice on our behalf was what pleased God so much that anyone can be reconciled by it. But people mistake the representation as Christ not being us and him dying instead of us, when really, instead of saying "substitutionary atonement," people should try saying just "the atonement," and know that if the cross counted for us at all, it means that Christ was us. Try that too-- instead of "Jesus loves you," "Jesus was you." Then there can be the love restored because you are now a perfect son of God. Anyway, it is kind of confusing, but all I know is that the theology that people fight over is true. And sometimes it just seems like people are always saying there is something else to believe and whatever you already think is not good enough, but really it is the opposite of that. If it is not making sense, try flipping it around. Instead of "nothing we can do is good enough," try, "of course it is good enough and we do not have to be perfect." You really can see the opposite thing almost at all times, and some teachers and preachers have a way of telling people the opposite thing every time, no matter how it flickers, they say the thing that makes you feel inadequate, when really you could be baptized by the Holy Spirit as soon as you see that you are not just a son of God but the son of God, beyond what any schizophrenic has ever said when they say they are Jesus Christ.

    "Behold the lamb of God, that takes away the sins of the world." John 1:29.

Fire Alarms

Something that is most painful to me is embarrassing, loud, or just bad music, especially in public places, and especially when you can't escape from it. A lot of places near where I live now in New York play loud music or embarrassing music where it almost sounds like a recording of people scrogging. It truly burns my mind and soul, and that was one of the things they did to me where I worked in a bookstore and they tried to get me to quit. I think some of my sensitivity is from autism, and a lot of it has to do with meaning. So if it were a more neutral loud noise I would be better off, but the meaning hurts me and they know it. I think a lot of the corporate people who choose music for their companies also know it, and that is part of their motivation, possibly to maintain power of some sort, or to have the power to repel employees and customers with morals. But anyway, I just want to look on the bright side for a moment and say that I think there is one benefit to it, which it is that it is kind of a public announcement that there are a lot of bad people in power in our country. People can say it is all about Trump, but I know that there are bad people all over the place in different professions, and we can see the corruption in a lot of ways. In my hometown, there is a hospital that sharkily bought out all the medical offices all around the region and is paying its employees less so they can use their money to eat up all the other medical places. How horrible. A lot of everyone's health care and even life is in some of these people's hands. But only to a certain extent, and what people have forgotten is that God is still in charge. Anyway, what I am saying is that all the nasty music that people think no one "sees" for what it is, is actually just a self-sabotaging announcement that a lot of bad people have gained power and intend to abuse people as they go about their most daily normal business of survival, and even if they just want to buy some cake mix and paper towels, they will be suffering a form of sexual abuse. Everyone will answer for it, and we have people in our culture who on Judgement Day will be charged with 300 million counts of things, and harm that literally hundreds of thousands of children will not recover from in this life.

Some people have told themselves that they will get a reward for certain destructive activism, but they will find out that their damage to the country will more likely cost thousands of hungry people in other countries their only chance for a meal. I am grieved every day by it, totally devastated, but as I feel the pain of shamings when I go in almost any store or even office supply place, I can be thankful that at least people have let us know beforehand what their intent for society is. It is to humiliate and ruin lives, and we now have the warning we need to prepare.

Extra Koala Post

Sorry everyone, but I want to say one more post about the koalas needing rain and water as fast as possible which is that I have started to think that not enough is being done and we should not be this reactive to things but should act faster and with more people, organize with email and other communication, and rescue the people and animals from disasters. Their country is burning. It could get worse and everyone should try to help in some way. I mean in real ways- not just saying "global warming, quick, flog an evangelical nearby." I am talking about rescues, kind of like when we see people giving an animal water, except there are hundreds of millions of animals who need that water. I don't see any news stories about hundreds of millions of animals being saved. 90,000 from Crocodile Hunter people, so that is good. But mostly I see one koala at a time on the news. I was quick to talk about religion in my other koala post, but there are things on earth that need our care always and immediately and that matter just as much.

The Law

Well everyone, I have one more post for this section which is about something I figured out several years ago when I tried to skim the whole Bible in a month. One section I read more carefully was the section with a lot of the ancient Jewish laws, which are often either rejected or used in arguments about religion and being gay. If you read those books, you can actually see that God was really looking out for people, and I think when people use those laws in discussions even about things like slavery, they also are missing some views and appreciation for how God consistently wanted for people to have freedom and fair wages. But to me, something interesting about the verses saying guys should not be persons with other guys or even that God "detests" people wearing clothes of the opposite gender, is that those verses actually might argue in favor of what people think of as gay marriage, in that they support being yourself and choosing the relationships that are real and most coordinated with your actual feelings of gender. In other words, for a gay person, a heterosexual marriage might be more like a gay marriage, and God does not want someone to be tortured for their whole life as they have to act out a relationship that they don't really feel. He would also be saying to dress in the way that really matches who you are. Hasn't everyone felt trapped before in a situation where you can't be yourself? Like if you had to dress up for church or a wedding and you couldn't wait to get back into your normal clothes? It is like that, and I think God wants people to have the right to be themselves and for any marriage or relationship to have the gender factor that he designed, which for many people will only work if they choose what seems to be biologically their same gender. Quickly I will add that what is psychological is often more biological than people realize, so people don't need to say that biology trumps psychology in any way. And in Christianity, there has often been a tradition of saying that the mind and heart should be in charge and have more say than the body anyway. So people really do have to be hypocrits when they insist on judging people for any reason that hides their true motivation of trying to establish themselves as superior in some way. That is all for now. I will include this in my book before posting it in my blog. Some people say that they don't care what the old laws say, but I do, and I find it very interesting if the whole law might hold up in some way some times, despite the fact that Paul in the New Testament gave everyone permission to disregard it if they wanted to. I also find it interesting if it turns out that those are the verses actually in most support of gay and trans rights, which is how I see them without a doubt.

Spirituality and Social Work Papers

Spiritual Journey

I am excited to be able to tell about some of my spiritual journey. A lot of it happens in my mind because I like to pray. I like to pray for strangers and brainstorm blessings to request for them and anyone else I can think of from associations starting with various people and groups of people. One of my current goals is to use maps more and try to pray for more people in other countries.

One of the reasons I pray a lot is because I was not successful in other ways, both as a religious person and as a person in society trying to be productive. I became severely mentally ill in college and from then on had a priority of mainly staying alive. A lot of good things that happen to me end up being a type of psychological food to help me endure the next stretch of time instead of being part of a stable framework of my life that I can depend on.

I grew up in South Carolina and my mom and dad took me and my sister to a Presbyterian Church downtown every week. We had a nice life and my mom and dad did the best they could to help us get a good start. I think they did a great job except for the way my mom oddly tried to squelch some friendships with people who she felt that I loved too much.

From the very beginning of my life, I found that I had a special ability to make people laugh, and it was my favorite thing to do. Especially in middle school, my humor was appreciated by a lot of people and I can still remember my friends' smiles and laughs. I was able to sometimes make whole classes laugh at one time, and when I could, it was a happiness like nothing else I could imagine.

In seventh grade, I went to camp with my church and was having a great time. I started writing funny poems about all my friends. The camp people told us about Jesus Christ and with the help of some friends, I decided that I believed it and needed to stop making fun of people and cursing. The cursing was not that bad of a problem but I did it for some kind of entertainment satisfaction and I knew that I could do better. When I went back to school in the fall, I did not curse anymore and when I thought of the funny jokes that hurt people, I would not say it. I would let the opportunity pass without getting the laughs. I still tried to be funny in other ways and made fun of teachers.

In high school I felt love from my church youth group and started learning to go beyond not making fun of people and start trying to help people through community service and reaching out to people I might not have otherwise been friends with. My youth group went on mission trips and the same people who had been in charge of that other camp told us more about Jesus Christ and described what happened on the cross. My parents did not like the religious influence even though they had been the ones to take us to church. They tried to control me to be normal, and I think they also tried to keep me out of environments with any kind of love because they knew I had a gender problem and they were scared that I would act on it. But I was far from doing that and just wanted to help people find out about Jesus Christ.

But I did not have the same rapport with people as I had in middle school and early high school. People saw a lack of love in my life from not expressing my gender in relationship, and when that guardedness and discipline was combined with a lifestyle of achievement and volunteering, people started hating me. I became a Young Life leader in college with a mission of sharing Christianity with high schoolers, but I had a nervous breakdown and left that group of friends in order to keep myself from being in that state of mind again. I knew I was in a survival situation and I worked hard by myself to focus on positive things and find friends that I was not tempted to manipulate as potential converts. God helped me and I was able to graduate. But right before the end of college, I was on a field trip to New York City and had a manic episode that had been building up for several weeks. I left my group and walked around New York in a psychotic state and then miraculously turned up at

Bellevue hospital in the middle of the night. It was in the newspapers, and my church that I had been going to in college was not happy about it and taught a Sunday School lesson when I got back, saying "Insanity is sin." But I knew I had done nothing wrong.

When I finished college, I went back to my hometown and was put on psychiatric medicine that sedated me and caused deep emotional pain. No one knew it could have been better, so I just took it every day. It ruined my life.

Despite the drugged state I was in, I got a job at Barnes and Noble and stayed there for twelve years. I learned to be a more honest person when I was there, and I had chronic religion problems from a fear that my religion might not be true as well as a fear that it was true and that the people nicest to me were going to go to hell.

But as I prayed a lot, I became more hopeful. I think about Judgement Day a lot and might try to be a lawyer for some of the court cases or have a game show to help people get their rewards. I also feel that I have gotten some of the blessings I have prayed for because I had good experiences in school programs and I learned how to write funny poetry.

I mentioned in class that the monk archetype has helped me survive and feel a sense of purpose. Another current archetype that is most helpful for me is the idea of a "schizophrenic prophet." I have always thought mental illness and mental hospitals were so awesome and even with all of my problems, I am overjoyed to be a psychiatric patient. I have all the symptoms I could ever want from just about every disorder there is.

Last year I participated in an online program at Princeton Seminary and I saw that the theology about the atonement and Christ's death is true. About a week after finally understanding it, I discovered that I had a new meditation gift of some kind. I would feel a feeling of fullness when I thought certain thoughts or was in a certain location. I did not know what it was and wondered if I had discovered some kind of Eastern spirituality that I needed to avoid in order to be loyal to my own religion. But then I felt the feeling again while walking near Wall Street at night, and I realized that it was the Holy Spirit. It is a baptism of the Holy Spirit like what a lot of Pentecostals experience. Sometimes I feel it a lot and sometimes I don't notice it. I am really excited about it because if I lose more of my mental strength, even to the point of not knowing anything, I will still have the holy spirit helping me do what is right. That is also a dream come true for me. There is a short story called "A Worn Path," about an old lady named Phoenix who has to get medicine for her grand-son and she can't see and is kind of out of it but is still able to make a hike a long way out of a faithful habit. There was also a lady I met in Jamaica on one of the mission trips and she had dementia and was tied to a bench but when I sat with her, she drew a purple cross. I always thought that kind of life was amazing and could only happen if God really did help you or include you in his help for others. I think now I might have opportunities like that.

I also want to share this idea which is that I think some of our guardian angels might be friendly imaginary animals that write kind reports about us for Judgement Day, kind of like these animals from online: (photo credit candy crush, etc)

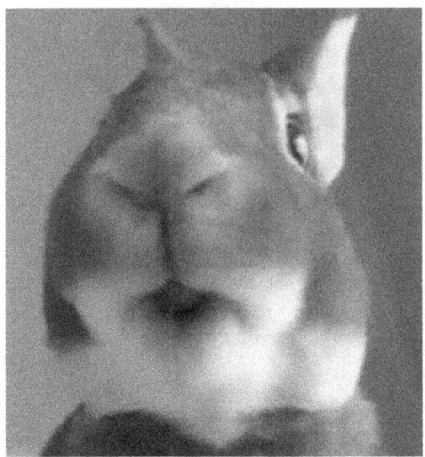

Journal Entry 2

The tradition that I belong to is Christianity. It is the best tradition there is because it has to do with going to heaven, where everyone will be happy. It also is a tradition where God does not turn down anyone who wants to be his friend. Literally no one is denied at all unless they are bad enough to snub their whole face and life at a suffering savior who died for them. If they have even a flicker of recognition that they are a sinner and might need forgiveness, Jesus Christ is willing to save them even though his life ended while being tortured by representatives of all of humanity. Jesus said he was building a mansion with many rooms. On the cross, when he said, "It is finished," he could have been referring to that mansion. It could have been a house that he built for his secret society family, or it could have been a mindfulness statement about the cross, saying that he accepted reality so much that the cross was a great mansion made from his own carpentry skills, and he was content to live there in those moments because of his great love. However, if I do not have a room in a literal mansion in heaven, I will be seeing Jesus Christ and many of his disciples in court.

Anyway, in trying to describe the reasons why I am happy to be a part of my religious tradition, it is hard to know whether to focus on the beliefs and believers, or to focus simply on God himself and reality, which would include Christianity as a religion within creation. People could say that the tradition itself includes God, Jesus, all the angels, all the people, and all of reality, so that the problems I have with my tradition could be things like world poverty, all suffering, or nothing at all because anything that God has ordained is what is best for everyone. But I think I will go ahead and view my tradition as being a religion within God's reality, and a tradition that might only overlap partially with what Jesus refers to in the New Testament as "the kingdom of God." He said the kingdom of God is within you, and he compared it to a mustard seed, and said it was like yeast that was worked through the dough. I would like to say that is my religious tradition, and in some of my memories, life is just like that. But I also imagine Christianity to have to do with faith, prayer, friends who also know about God and trust him with their lives, and a whole history of saints and sinners and workers and soldiers who have done all kinds of glorious things and terrible things in God's name. I have sometimes felt surrounded by people who love to find fault in all of it, but I definitely am thankful to be part of Christianity, and I see it essentially as total forgiveness and admission to a literal heaven where everyone will be happy and good all the time. There will be no lying, no child abuse, no fear of having our lives ruined, and no pain. Things are not like that right now, so there is a perpetual philosophical conundrum to try to understand. But it is not that difficult. Either the bad people won't be bad anymore, or they will not be in heaven. I am happy with that deal, even as an imperfect sinner, and I have concluded that Jesus Christ was telling the truth when he promised eternal life and salvation for anyone who asks or even just believes.

Something from my evangelical background that I don't understand has to do with how necessary faith is. Worrying about people's salvation and everyone's experience on Judgement Day has been a torment that has lasted pretty much my entire life since becoming a Christian in middle school. But as I work it out in my mind and find love and peace by being friends with other caring people, the theological conundrums sometimes become entertaining and I am able to write funny poems that make the trouble all worth it. That is just my experience, and if people I know end up screaming and humiliated as they disappear into a lake of fire, then I don't know what all will be worth what. I live with that burden every day and pray for everyone, looking for opportunities to share what I know to anybody who seems like they would not be mad to hear some good news about something that has to do with free food and love forever.

As I try to think of the negative things about Christianity, some of our societal problems are obvious, and yet I know so well that just about everyone I know who professes Christian faith would have been much worse without it. Our religion is not really the problem. The problem is people's same sins as usual, and anyone who has taken up the fight against their own evil is way more likely to defeat it then the people who watch and criticize as they do whatever they can to fill their hundred greedy stomachs that crave death and shame.

Anyway, I sound mad and sometimes am because people have been mean to me. I should have spent my patience working to provide food for the hungry and sharing extra love and knowledge instead of just enduring a whole culture's offensive assault on decency, on good people, and on the greatness behind those people, which turns out to be God himself. Sometimes it seems that the reward for any triumph and loyalty in my heart is to be overwhelmed with grief for all the suffering that could have been prevented if everyone took that one step of faith that evangelicals try to sell. But I think I could be surprised some day, and in purgatory it will turn out that what I really wanted was to beat everyone at anything, and several hundred million people were willing to play along.

Journal Entry 3

Today I read in our textbook about different religions, and then read the chapter about creating a spiritually sensitive context for practice. Our journal assignment is supposed to be based on chapter 7, but after reading both sections, I thought that the descriptions of the traditions on their own seemed more authentic than the application of some of those systems to the environment and models of social work practice described in chapter 7. I wanted to note that observation because it could be relevant to what the ideal implementation of the wisdom for social work that is available in people's religious backgrounds, beliefs, and especially from the reality they are aware of or loyal to.

First of all, I think that social workers in general seem to have done really well in helping people with all of their needs, including spiritual needs, and I think the social work field itself has come about from years of collaboration from people who really cared. I think that kind of caring has already won out over all and will continue to do so as much as people sincerely try to help anyone else who suffers. The survey article was a sign of that, even with such low numbers of social workers from a few minority religions, and I think even in a quest for diversity, people should not doubt too much the wisdom behind the code of ethics and the traditions of empathy and intervention that have already emerged and helped millions of people. There might be a philosophical task at hand to consider that diverse wisdom might not clash with itself, and that if there is some kind of exclusion, discrimination, or conflict affecting clients or workers, then it is from some kind of misunderstanding or bias that should not be automatically attributed to anyone's spiritual background.

This is where I see a different alternative to the integration of spirituality into social work environments than what is described in the textbook. I thought that the imposition of the yin and yang idea as part of the conceptual model of "holistic" social work was superficial, and a little hypocritical after most social workers have been taught to keep personal beliefs out of their interaction with clients. Also, though I am not currently employed in the social work field anywhere, I think the challenge of decisions made and services provided by most mental health organizations is far beyond using other religions as some kind of theme for organizational culture. I think all it would do is set up people to violate their own beliefs by having to offer some kind of cooperation and agreement with things they don't believe in order to keep their jobs and help people.

Also, I don't mean this to be flattering, but the circle of insight paradigm does not strike me in the same way, and I think it has more potential to offer both practicioners and clients a way to really share and draw from their most deeply held values and motivations.

The other main strategy I think could be a way of making the most of spirituality within organizations is to expand counseling components of social work and allow individual social workers, mental health workers, and case workers to fully be themselves and offer their truest assessments and insights based on any background resource they have, whether it has to do with knowledge, identity, or faith and relationship. As proven as therapy strategies have been, there are a lot of people who do want counseling of various sorts, and being equipped to sincerely offer one's true perspective that is limited in a good way could be an opportunity for agencies to incorporate all of the wisdom and resources for healing that are available. A lot of social work places and therapists already do that, but in a culture where social identity matters so much to people, going ahead and letting people function fully as their true selves would probably be one way of increasing spiritual resources that are both diverse and authentic.

The chapter did not rile me up, but when I think about people foisting on people one of these religions that uses ideas about holistic healing and being one with a universe that actually has some stuff you should not be one with, instead of actually letting people be themselves and offer everything they have to help everyone they can, I do get a little bit mad. I think it is a false vision of wholeness and clients will see it for what it is. People who already are depressed and anxious should not have to be patiently humoring professionals who are paid to save their lives.

The other issue I had with these chapters were the comments about moving away from strategies that had to do with intervention. I think that intervention is the truest manifestation of the love mentioned early in the chapter, which was translated as caring and empathy. A lot of people have problems they need more than listening for, and workers and volunteers who do other types of service like signing people up for benefits, providing food, legal services, activism, and all kinds of other service, should be seen as integral, and all effective intervention as a moral necessity and a high level of care. I think that if this does not happen, then the only true social workers will be whoever kills the traffickers.

I kind of want to end my paper there, but I have one other thought to add, which is that I think the gist of what could be improved for spirituality and social work is a removal of gags instead of an imposition of more gags, or even worse, puppetry where people are forced to act out other religions they don't believe in just to participate and offer the fraction of the true care they are still allowed to offer.

Journal Entry 4

I think I might not be able to achieve the organizational smoothness that the topics from this weeks' chapters deserve, so I am going to just start with my main reaction to several statements from these readings, which is that sometimes I feel sorry for people who look down on me and other religious people, no matter how low we are on society's totem pole. The article about engaging in dialogue with people who genuinely have different beliefs has some great ideas, and they mainly match an approach that I have embraced and lived by. However, when I read the author's final zinging conclusion that sometimes people just need to sit down and shut up, I know who he is talking to, and I feel bad for him. And while Canda, whose ideas I mostly appreciate, actually suggests the ridiculous claim that it may be unethical to pray for people without their consent, I think the real ethical issue that people don't think they have to contend with is how far the consideration and polite appreciation for other beliefs can go before it becomes pretense, or really, just a lie, that should also be in question.

Would Muslims see it the same way I do, or Buddhists? I do not know. But I think that something educated people often can't understand is that people really do believe their beliefs. Christians who are supposedly the most guilty of promoting beliefs in settings that need to be welcoming and inclusive have often been more accommodating and patient then they are given credit for. And this other question that is emerging in my mind is whether it is really credit they should get for that in the first place, or if that kind of compliance and withholding of spiritual knowledge is in fact the more ethically questionable thing.

The implications of how much spirituality to personally express as a social worker could be very broad and very detailed at the same time. Even within five minutes of a session, should a therapist or counselor choose total nonjudgemental acceptance or confront someone in a lie? Should a therapist feel authorized to help a client figure out what is false guilt from depression versus what really might be a true lifelong haunting from actual wrongdoing? And if a therapist is wielding some kind of continual resource from years of sunday school and knows the client could have all that and more with just a slight adjustment in religious thinking, is it really acceptable to keep them from accepting it? Maybe the rules of social work can set everyone free from the torturesome burden of having to figure out when to share what, but if it were simpler and everyone just told whatever truth they knew could be beneficial, there might not be as many conundrums as people might expect.

There is some life-saving and soul saving stuff in people's religious beliefs, and while I think some of these things are already such an objective part of life that social workers already use a lot of the best ethics in almost everything they do, the kind of silence about faith that is often recommended and definitely supported in these readings could represent a lost opportunity on a mass societal scale.

I do not know how all the statistics of our society's poverty, homelessness, and mental illness line up, but lost faith in the lives of individuals and the larger society is likely to take a tragic toll and is one reason that I think social workers should be careful about trying to allow expression of some religions and not others. If there is an impulse to even things out by giving some of the minority religions a voice and expecting politeness from the religions who already had their two hundred years of fame, or more like 2000 years of veracity, then people might need to ask themselves what the real motivation and benefit of that plan is. And in that discussion, I think possibly the most relevant factors to consider are not actual religious views but psychological habits and defenses that might explain why so many people want to create a culture where people have to deny very well proven beliefs in order to supposedly not hurt anyone. Is there maybe something about religion that offends people more than the mistakes like gender discrimination? Is the real problem maybe that people feel outdone or exposed in their own meaningless or selfish habits?

The dialogue article literally suggests a patient silence, which also happens to be one of the main accusations I hear in the media towards conservatives or maybe just evangelicals. And when I see both the accusation of people being silent at the wrong time and not silent at the right time, then I have to wonder if what some people want is just to be in charge and use us all to seem like they made a difference that they didn't but could have.

The other issue that I want to come back to is a question of how much religions should have equal status as part of a dialogue, as opposed to people having equal status in dialogue and being able to say what they really believe. Using the example of Canda saying it could be unethical to pray for someone without their consent, I could think of a scenario where a witch client might say they were casting spells to benefit me. Do I say that is their choice, or do I ask them not to do that because of my own beliefs? This is where to me I do not have to say that a sorcery spell has equal weight as a prayer. I can say whatever I want to and they can do whatever they want to. The religion wins out in both cases. An actual example from a spirituality group I led as an intern is when someone seemed mad that I brought in the Beatitudes from the Bible for discussion. It has a verse that I think is relevant to treating addiction, which is "Blessed are they who hunger and thirst for righteousness, for they shall be filled." If people can't tolerate being in a group where multiple things are shared and that is one of them, no matter who brings it in, I feel sorry for them and that is where I draw the line in my own participation in this embarrassing charade of modern life where we all pretend that God has not yet saved the world.

Journal Entry 5

This morning I am having to skip some volunteer work because of not feeling good. I had some physical pain triggered by emotional stress. I got cut from a volunteer shift bagging groceries, possibly because I mumbled too much while volunteering last time. I was mad because people kept getting in my way on purpose. I know they were doing it, and that place has done it a lot, but I have been patient. But sometimes it seems motivated by some kind of social justice activism, or an attempt at turning a volunteer shift into a racial skit of some kind for the clients, and a power play against volunteers who might seem overconfident while reaching for rice and beans to fill grocery bags. Anyway, as I felt sad about possibly not being able to go to my favorite volunteer place anymore, I started feeling terrible abdominal pain. It is just cramps but I had to have an online appointment.

Today I am going to order some breakfast and work on my novel. It is a kids book about an English teacher and some imaginary mice. I am finishing it pretty fast. I think it will end up being the second book in a trilogy. Then I will come to social work class. I am a little bit worried about the meditation but I will probably stay in the room and pray, no matter what the person does for the meditation.

The reading about assessment was very interesting, and I mostly found it to be either helpful or talking about things beyond what I can currently do. I have recently been feeling discouraged about social work and thinking also that I might want to retreat from New York and go be an evangelical in the south.

But probably I will stay here. I think the main assessment challenge for me has to do with staying nonjudgemental but addressing client habits that I think could be harmful in some way. Maybe this is something I have always managed in working with all people, but I have always felt like it was a weakness for me to successfully confront people who are not doing what they are supposed to. And assessment is part of that. How much should we acknowledge evil for what it is, even if it seems to just be like some kind of extra edge of anger or neglect of some kind, and how much is unconditional acceptance always the secret to helping people genuinely aspire to be their best self in service of others? I genuinely don't know, and think I err on the side of acceptance, which is probably part of the reason I have made my way to the social work field. But I have cop and soldier inclinations, too.

Anyway, those are my genuine wrestlings with the material, though I still have leftover grumbles from last week's articles that to me had a slight but obvious anti-evangelical and anti-conservative bias. I think that with all the beliefs and resentments about "privilege" and "Christian privilege" that are so prevalent and driving in social work influenced communities, to not see the justice of evangelicals wanting to not be the only elite saved to heaven by themselves, and to take the effort to share their faith in almost any way with people who didn't get the same Sunday school training as them, is pretty hypocritical and an embarrassing shame.

Adding this later: Sorry for the negativity. Also, it turns out that I wasn't cut from the volunteer project and it was really canceled because of some kind of scheduling reason.

Journal 6

This journal is about the chapters on how to promote spiritual growth in clients. I thought the book chapters were very interesting and helpful, and I thought that the inclusion of helping clients forgive was especially helpful. I think that is a very meaningful spiritual goal for clients who are trying to cope and endure problems or move past difficult set-backs ranging from general mistreatment and lack of appreciation all the way to horrific abuse.

And I think something to keep in mind relates to what Dudley referred to as overzealous workers or clients, and that has to do with an impatience and rush towards the forgiveness when there may need to be more of a sense of justice and recognition of people's wrongdoing for a long time before a client can do the truly worthy and relief-giving acts of forgiveness.

I think that is also where an activism component comes in, and a question of whether workers are doing everything they can in general to help their society offer justice to people in all contexts. I guess once people are part of the social work field, then they are probably in that kind of full-time work. But I think that there is spiritual and mental work that people can do where they vigilantly maintain a certain responsibility and habit to defend oppressed people and include anyone who needs an extension of patience and outreach for the sake of making sure all people have all the various kinds of food and shelter that they need. And before I support too much that social workers have automatically signed up for that, I have to say that social workers and therapists are often paid by insurance, and that system is destroying lives and has been for about thirty years. So it might not be as much automatic game-over just from participation and adherence to the code of ethics within the profession.

But that is not the main thing I want to mention in this journal. The main thing I want to say has to do with something surprising I think about spiritual growth. It matches something else I think about mental health, which is that having a job or a happy and successful school experience can be more important for people's recovery and for their life experience in general than almost any amount of mental health treatment or care. And I think that can also be said about spiritual growth. I think that the most powerful resource within the school and work solutions for mental illness or other life struggles may be the gift of mentorship from regular people who have roles of teaching, leadership, friendship, coworker interactions, or even just basic existence as an acquaintance in someone's community.

There is growth that happens from caring relationships, especially when there is some form of superiority in terms of age, knowledge or experience. I use the word "superiority" in the etiquette sense and not as a value judgement. I use it like someone would try to view someone as a "superior," as they decide what to call someone or what choice of behavior to use. Anyway, many social work and therapy relationships are meant to provide that, and it is a great burden that people come through on as their job. But I think that no one should lose sight of the fact that clients may also benefit from other community people in a similar way, and that just as mental health strengthening may come from other sources, spiritual or religious guidance and example doesn't have to happen from official church sources either.

Some of my heroes who made a difference in my life were my bosses at my old bookstore job. People could question how spiritual the growth was, but I would say that there is a spiritual component always present in most interactions, and in most of life. And as I did what I was supposed to under their direction and benefited from their example of kindness and work, I maintained or increased my own habits of treating people well and doing what seemed best in all work situations.

That kind of provision could seem outside of a social workers scope of practice or influence, but I think that as anything can be discussed in a session, all the life opportunities for spiritual growth are things that social workers can help clients find and try not to lose.

Journal 7

The chapter I read today was about spiritual growth. There was a chart about getting through times that become chaotic and then stabilize. It was similar to a framework that involves stages or phases. I would say it is the material that most lost me so far. I have no understanding of it whatsoever. Its connection to a religion is irrelevant. What I see in it is a way of graphing some expected chain of events or process that a person might go through as they face things in life that they do not understand. But I think that this mold presented just can't reflect anyone's situation in a reliable way. I guess people map out crisis situations all the time, and that is how things like the "stages of grief" are discovered. But this is where I think as a client and think, these people just do not understand what some people experience. They do not know the level of crisis, of abuse that encompasses the depths of complete meaninglessness in its injustice, and to think that any of it can be understood as some kind of normal part of life is just ludicrous.

The chapter mentioned some other social work understandings, and narrative therapy is one of them. I think that the narrative component is what best combats an unresonant application of some standard growth map, though to me what is considered narrative therapy sometimes discards the true benefits of narrative understanding and encourages people to make up narratives that in the end will not provide the deepest healing and acceptance.

My reaction is interesting to me because it reminds me of how I would go to church a lot and knew that really it was for sane people. The music was comforting, and the leaders did everything they could for me as a mentally ill person except for their hidden discriminatory views and lack of understanding. But I knew that the sermons were designed for more common suffering, and were mostly helping healthy people achieve more and succeed at being better than everyone who was brutally attacked by the world and the devil, and who had to manage weaknesses and pain that were beyond what made sense to talk about in sermons.

    Spirituality does reach into those depths, and stories in the Bible are full of wisdom and love for any of the most unheard of, unrecognized, and uncared for tragedies and chronic difficulties. But some people who have vocations to lead good people to be better, have to shake off the suffering weak people sometimes in order to help their mainstream core people reach the heights. And this might not be inappropriate on some levels. For social workers helping people who might be going through something that fits in well to a map of how life works, these spiritual frameworks might work well.

    But I have to conclude that my impulse to not spend that much time puzzling over it, but instead to just see it immediately as another resource for the healthy people, is probably somewhat accurate. I also again find myself thinking that a superficial mastery and application of spiritual concepts to a client's case is not the task at hand, and that it is within the actual tradition and fellowship and deep, complex truth of a whole worldview that clients can find the spiritual resources available to them.

    Something that I don't dismiss as easily and could think about for much longer is how some of the main therapies and social work strategies can still help clients endure sufferings and heartbreak and find relief from some of the most agonizing and confusing situations. It is also an area for professional development for me, so I only know a little bit of what I mean.

    One more thing is to say philosophically something about what the Rabbi speaker last time was talking about complicated grief. I think that it is an interesting topic to think about what kind of grief is normal, and the nature of grief. Some grief is a normal part of life, and can almost be a happy kind of sadness. And some grief is over things that a lot of people will just never understand in their health and normalcy. The chasm between that kind of life and the life of people who suffer with no comfort can't be captured in ideas about privilege, or even discrimination. Some understandings of abuse start to approach the truth of it, but eventually people will probably have to see that the wisdom is in the pain itself, and for all the people who want to meditate and find some peace of mind based on accepting reality as it is, sheer pain might be the more insightful meditation.

Journal 8

This chapter on nonsectarian belief and existentialism was really excellent and I really appreciated how Canda phrased and labeled various ideas and conceptualized atheism and other ways of understanding that were not religiously affiliated.

I think there is so much to learn from atheists, and I have thought before how atheists can make good social workers because they believe it could be all up to them to help someone and aren't as tempted to just hope for the best and rely on supernatural intervention. That could be bad for me to say, as if I myself don't believe that God would help people and is not trustworthy to save people from the kind of pits mentioned elsewhere in the book, but I think that there is something to be said for not lazily and blindly getting too dependent on religion in some way, and atheists often don't do that.

I think there is a risk, though, of any divide of sacred and secular, and in this case, atheists can walk away with the "ownership" of things in life that aren't as often designated as "spiritual." It is kind of like a flip side of Gnosticism, where some theologians tried to say that in the Lord's prayer, "Give us this day our daily bread," was only referring to some kind of spiritual food.

Really, there are all kinds of resources to try to make sure any client can benefit from, and I think social workers are often the ones most likely to try to help people who have lacked something to try to recover it, whether it is a religious client who doesn't have enough human relationships, or an atheist who might have missed out on some spiritual growth or community and fellowship.

But atheists to me almost provide a spiritual and social experiment for the whole world to learn from, where people can see their views and lives and speculate about what if what we see on earth really was all there is. I am using the term atheist instead of existentialist, even though I liked that word choice in the book. But I think that it is also kind of weird for people who don't believe in God to get to use the theme of "existing." I think in extreme forms those terms can be used aggressively to try to minimize the presence of people of different faiths.

People can say that is the whole point and the religious people already got enough societal benefits and affirmation, but I think that is an example of some of a very real bias against some religions and people.

Anyway, I have once again veered towards religious tangents that usually end up claiming that Christians are persecuted, when that is not the whole story and kind of off topic from the social work issues that I need to improve on.

If I see the task as needing to know how to provide care for atheists, I would say that I feel more secure with that population than others for some reason, and have always loved atheists, with Ayn Rand and Isaac Asimov being two of my favorites, and Carl Sagan falling short of intellectual success in my mind. I also have read a book called "The Case against God," by George Smith, that clarifies an absence of belief instead of just an aggression against "believers." Some people have simply not organized their lives around something they can't see, and there is an honesty to it that should not be taken for granted.

I think one challenge for me could come at the end of someone's life if I were a chaplain who believes there is a real risk in not officially signing up for God's salvation, but I think that I would handle it like I have tried to handle situations all my life and just say whatever I felt was most helpful, with a knowledge and assurance that the guts it takes to be an atheist in our society is so much like trust in God that it could turn out to be the more strong "saving faith."

5.1 A religious tradition other than my own: Judaism

I identify as being almost all sections of Christianity, including Orthodox and Catholic, and I go to a church where they have an even more universal outlook than I do. So I felt that I could not stay within my main religion for this assignment because any option would count as my own perspective. But when I considered attending a service that is not my perspective, I sometimes felt that my attendance could be considered a form of participation on some levels. I would still consider going somewhere, like to a Buddhist place or Mosque, but I decided that my best option was to go to a synagogue.

Well then I still felt hesitant and the synagogue that I chose had closed offices on the day I needed to get permission. And I just felt like too much of an intruder. But I have actually gone to a synagogue twice in recent months to volunteer at a gathering for Holocaust survivors. I have decided to use the most recent experience there for this assignment. I hope that is okay. My belief is that the Jewish people have both a religious identity and a racial identity, and that they are persecuted for both reasons. I read a book once called "Why the Jews," and it explained some theories about Jewish persecution. It talked about how they sometimes are persecuted because people resent them for being blessed by God, and other times it could be other reasons. I think of course it has to do with both religion and racism, and most of all I think it has to do with a reason for so much persecution, which is against people who do what they are supposed to. In the Beatitudes, Jesus says "Blessed is he who is persecuted for righteousness, for theirs is the kingdom of heaven." I do not think it is coincidence that the topic of persecution is mentioned in that context as being related to righteousness. In the book of Hebrews in the Bible, there is discussion about righteousness being credited to Abraham because of faith. So faith could also make people targets. The loss of faith that happens in horrible events like the Holocaust is also reason to believe that religion would be a factor behind the persecution.

Anyway, I only know a certain amount about the Holocaust and I think it will be a while before I can read more and really think again about what happened to people. But it is really something to learn from in so many ways, so I think I will.

My contact for going to the gathering, which is an occasional lunch for Holocaust survivors and their caregivers and others, was a person named Lisa who has worked in human resources for the ad agency called Saatchi and Saatchi. That is the best agency there is, and she is like a celebrity to me. She and some staff people from a group called "----" told us some about the gathering and the people there and said that some people had to flee the Nazis, some people had to hide from the Nazis, and some people were in the concentration camps.

At the event, the other volunteers and I brought food to the tables, and helped serve coffee and tea. It was a tough social challenge in front of everyone, with some awkward interactions. There seemed to also be a role playing aspect to it where at times we had the role of being perceived as Nazis. It was kind of rough but I think for me the greater challenge was feeling a little bit of my gender struggles which happens at nice occasions where I am being perceived in a certain way that makes me feel like a particular psychological pain of insecurity. It had to do with people being dressed up in a synagogue and me wearing the bandana that I always wear and really have to wear now because I usually cut my own hair and don't really have the option of not wearing the bandana. I also could not wear my sunglasses which protect me from intrusive thoughts that are made worse by shamings.

But I know that the people there more than anyone probably understand suffering and injustice so much that I did not need to feel like they were hurting me like other society problems have hurt me before.

Anyway I don't need to go on and on about it but it was one of the main parts of the experience for me to have those feelings again when I thought I had escaped that 7 years ago and would never have to even dress nicely again because of being a poet.

Something else very striking about being in the synagogue location was that in the nice social room we were in, the walls were all mirrors, so you would look around and imagine the having three times as many people there and see a crowd of reflections that served as a reminder of how much more people should have been there or not been there. I say "not been there," because the people there should not have been hurt either.

Getting to go to that social event was definitely a special thing in my whole life that I do not really feel worthy of but also feel thankful for because I do care about Judaism, Jewish people, and the Holocaust. I also think that even though I feel that this kind of gathering, which has at least some religious components, seems different enough from my own to write about, the Bible says that Christians were "grafted in" to the branches of Judaism like a plant. So to me, Jewish people were the original children of God, and if I am also a child of God, then it is not really a different religion.

Theologically, I have to wonder where the cross is in the Old Testament, and I have recently considered that it might have to do with the statement that God is a jealous God. Legitimate jealousy is so horrible, and I could imagine that whatever causes God to feel that way might be related to the ultimate suffering that was revealed and experienced on the cross.

That is a little impositional to end my paper with, but I think something everyone has in common is that we don't know the cost behind our own existence and God's patience with us, and especially forgiveness.

This reminds me to say one more thing, which is that the quote at the beginning of this chapter caught my eye:

> You will never attain piety until you spend out of what you hold dear, and whatever you may spend of anything, Allah indeed knows it.
>
> —The Qur'an (3:92), Islam

I do not call God by that name, but this quote really makes sense to me and I could never disregard it as not being true or relevant to anyone. I have felt for years that I could not offer Muslims the consideration of reading their texts because of my terrible religion problems and proneness to confusion. But I read that quote and feel strong enough to navigate Islam more than I had planned. So that is a great sign of progress and relief. I mention it because it is another interesting experience with another religion, and helps me see just a glimpse of an extent to which probably almost everyone has some concept of certain things and at the same time, the lack of concept that can serve always as a promise of future joy to keep learning and understanding.

Refried Bean lives in NYC with three pet guinea pigs named Fred, Roger, and Dave. Refried has an MFA from Vermont College of Fine Arts and an MSW from New York University.

www.ingramcontent.com/pod-product-compliance
Lightning Source LLC
Chambersburg PA
CBHW070652220526
45466CB00001B/411